MW00575373

Cherokee Nation v. Georgia

The Forced Removal of a People

by Nathan Aaseng

FAMOUS
TRIALS

Lucent Books, San Diego, CA

Titles in the Famous Trials series include:

The Boston Massacre
Brown v. Board of Education
The Dred Scott Decision
The Impeachment of Bill
Clinton
Miranda v. Arizona
The Nuremberg Trials
The O.J. Simpson Trial
Roe v. Wade

The Rosenberg Espionage
Case
The Salem Witch Trials
The Scopes Trial
The Trial of Adolf Eichmann
The Trial of Joan of Arc
The Trial of John Brown
The Trial of Socrates

Library of Congress Cataloging-in-Publication Data

Aaseng, Nathan.
   Cherokee Nation v. Georgia / by Nathan Aaseng.
     p. cm. — (Famous trials)
   Includes bibliographical references and index.
   Summary: Describes the attempts to protect the rights of Cherokees living in Georgia beginning in the colonial period, including the landmark Supreme Court cases, Cherokee Nation vs. Georgia, and Worcester vs. Georgia.
   ISBN 1-56006-628-8 (lib. bdg. : alk. paper)
   1. Cherokee Nation—Trials, litigation, etc.—Juvenile literature. 2. Georgia—Trials, litigation, etc.—Juvenile literature. 3. Cherokee Indians—Legal status, laws, etc.— Georgia—Juvenile literature. [1. Cherokee Indians—Trials, litigation, etc. 2. Cherokee Indians—Legal status, laws, etc. 3. Indians of North America—Georgia—Legal status, laws, etc.] I. Title: Cherokee Nation versus Georgia. II. Series.
KF228.C48 A17   2000
342.73'0872—dc21   99-045621
                                                  CIP

Table of Contents

Foreword   4

Introduction
A Question of Principles   7
Chapter 1
Cherokee Land   11
Chapter 2
Federal Policy: Civilize or Relocate?   27
Chapter 3
Cherokee Nation v. Georgia   42
Chapter 4
Worcester v. Georgia   58
Chapter 5
Results of the Cherokee Cases   72

Notes   86
For Further Reading   89
Works Consulted   90
Index   92
Picture Credits   96
About the Author   96

Foreword

"The law is not an end in and of itself, nor does it provide ends. It is preeminently a means to serve what we think is right."

William J. Brennan Jr.

THE CONCEPT OF JUSTICE AND THE RULE OF LAW are hallmarks of Western civilization, manifested perhaps most visibly in widely famous and dramatic court trials. These trials include such important and memorable personages as the ancient Greek philosopher Socrates, who was accused and convicted of corrupting the minds of his society's youth in 399 B.C.; the French maiden and military leader Joan of Arc, accused and convicted of heresy against the church in 1431; to former football star O.J. Simpson, acquitted of double murder in 1995. These and other well-known and controversial trials constitute the most public, and therefore most familiar, demonstrations of a Western legal tradition that dates back through the ages. Although no one is certain when the first law code appeared or when the first formal court trials were held, Babylonian ruler Hammurabi introduced the first known law code in about 1760 B.C. It remains unclear how this code was administered, and no records of specific trials have survived. What is clear, however, is that humans have always sought to govern behavior and define actions in terms of law.

Almost all societies have made laws and prosecuted people for going against those laws, but the question of which behaviors to sanction and which to censure has always been controversial and remains in flux. Some, such as Roman orator and legislator Cicero, argue that laws are simply applications of universal standards. Cicero believed that humanity would agree on what constituted illegal behavior and that human laws were a mere extension of natural laws. "True law is right reason in agreement with nature," he wrote,

4

world-wide in scope, unchanging, everlasting. . . . We may not oppose or alter that law, we cannot abolish it, we cannot be freed from its obligations by any legislature. . . . This [natural] law does not differ for Rome and for Athens, for the present and for the future. . . . It is and will be valid for all nations and all times.

Cicero's rather optimistic view has been contradicted throughout history, however. For every law made to preserve harmony and set universal standards of behavior, another has been born of fear, prejudice, greed, desire for power, and a host of other motives. History is replete with individuals defying and fighting to change such laws—and even to topple governments that dictate such laws. Abolitionists fought against slavery, civil rights leaders fought for equal rights, millions throughout the world have fought for independence—these constitute a minimum of reasons for which people have sought to overturn laws that they believed to be wrong or unjust. In opposition to Cicero, then, many others, such as eighteenth-century English poet and philosopher William Godwin, believe humans must be constantly vigilant against bad laws. As Godwin said in 1793:

Laws we sometimes call the wisdom of our ancestors. But this is a strange imposition. It was as frequently the dictate of their passion, of timidity, jealousy, a monopolizing spirit, and a lust of power that knew no bounds. Are we not obliged perpetually to renew and remodel this misnamed wisdom of our ancestors? To correct it by a detection of their ignorance, and a censure of their intolerance?

Lucent Books' *Famous Trials* series showcases trials that exemplify both society's praiseworthy condemnation of universally unacceptable behavior, and its misguided persecution of individuals based on fear and ignorance, as well as trials that leave open the question of whether justice has been done. Each volume begins by setting the scene and providing a historical context to show how society's mores influence the trial process and the verdict.

Each book goes on to present a detailed and lively account of the trial, including liberal use of primary source material such as direct testimony, lawyers' summations, and contemporary and modern commentary. In addition, sidebars throughout the text create a broader context by presenting illuminating details about important points of law, information on key personalities, and important distinctions related to civil, federal, and criminal procedures. Thus, all of the primary and secondary source material included in both the text and the sidebars demonstrates to readers the sources and methods historians use to derive information and conclusions about such events.

Lastly, each *Famous Trials* volume includes one or more of the following comprehensive tools that motivate readers to pursue further reading and research. A timeline allows readers to see the scope of the trial at a glance, annotated bibliographies provide both sources for further research and a thorough list of works consulted, a glossary helps students with unfamiliar words and concepts, and a comprehensive index permits quick scanning of the book as a whole.

The insight of Oliver Wendell Holmes Jr., distinguished Supreme Court justice, exemplifies the theme of the *Famous Trials* series. Taken from *The Common Law*, published in 1881, Holmes remarked: "The life of the law has not been logic, it has been experience." That "experience" consists mainly in how laws are applied in society and challenged in the courts, a process resulting in differing outcomes from one generation to the next. Thus, the *Famous Trials* series encourages readers to examine trials within a broader historical and social context.

Introduction

A Question of Principles

THE CHEROKEE WERE desperate. The white settlers of Georgia, no longer content with nibbling at the edges of the tribe's ancient homelands, had begun to openly grab Indian farmlands.

News of the latest humilating blow in Georgia's campaign to intimidate its native population spread quickly among the Cherokee in the summer of 1830. Soldiers from the state of Georgia had entered Cherokee territory and arrested George Tassels, a Cherokee accused of killing another tribe member on Cherokee land. According to treaties made with the U.S. government, the matter should have been left to the Cherokee government to decide. But Georgia had shoved aside the Cherokee government and taken over the case. The state court found Tassels guilty of murder and sentenced him to death.

The Tassels case was proof that the Georgia legislature meant what it said when it had declared all Cherokee laws invalid and had forbidden the tribe's government to meet. From now on, said the lawmakers, tribe members living on Cherokee land within the state of Georgia were subject to state laws.

Cruel Laws

Those laws were cruel—intended to make life so miserable for the Cherokee that they would leave their lands and move west. After gold was discovered in Cherokee territory in 1829, Indians were forbidden to dig on their own land. Georgia officials surveyed Cherokee land and divided it into parcels to be sold in the coming state land lottery. The Georgia government refused to acknowledge Cherokee ownership of their land, and refused to help the Cherokee keep the hundreds of prospectors from swarming onto their land. Some of the intruders kicked the Cherokee out of their homes, stole their livestock, and took over their farms.

The state created a special police force called the Georgia Guard to patrol Cherokee land. The Georgia Guard mistreated and terrorized Indians. They arrested Cherokee people for no reason, then charged them with disturbing the peace when they resisted these unfair arrests. They made cheap liquor available to the Cherokee, encouraged them to drink, and then arrested them for public disorder. The worst of the Georgia Guard set fire to Cherokee crops and then laughed as they watched the women frantically try to put out the fires.

The Cherokee refused to be provoked into violence. They appealed to the state courts for justice. But under Georgia law, Indians were not allowed to testify in court. Whites could commit any crime they pleased against Indians without fear of consequence unless a white person testified against them. The Cherokee appealed to the federal government to honor their promise to protect them. But President Andrew Jackson turned a deaf ear to their pleas. For a time, federal soldiers offered only token protection against the Georgia settlers' harrassment of the Cherokee. Then, at the request of the state of Georgia, the federal troops withdrew altogether.

One Last Chance

Some of those who sympathized with the Cherokee urged them to try one last avenue of justice. The Supreme Court was charged with final responsibility for maintaining justice in matters involving the federal government. Since Native American territories were guaranteed by treaties with the federal government, perhaps the Supreme Court would see to it that the treaties were enforced and the Cherokee treated fairly.

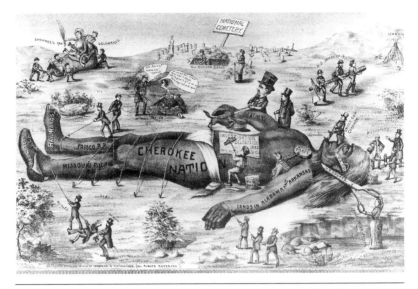

This mid-nineteenth century lithograph depicts the injustice that Native Americans were subjected to. The Cherokees inhabiting Georgia were forced to obey the cruel laws of the Georgia legislature.

The Cherokee were hesitant about treading on this unfamiliar ground. But when the Tassels situation came up, they asked a prominent attorney, William Wirt, to appeal the case to the Supreme Court. On December 12, 1830, the Supreme Court issued an order to Governor Gilmer of Georgia for the state to send representatives to respond to the Cherokee's complaint that the state was disregarding their rights.

Georgia officials, however, had no intention of letting the Supreme Court interfere with what they considered to be a state matter. Two days after receiving the Court's notice, Georgia hanged Tassels. With Tassels dead, the case could no longer be argued.

Although shocked by Georgia's grim response, the Cherokee did not give up. The Supreme Court had offered some encouragement by at least considering the Cherokee's complaint. Perhaps if they brought a formal complaint against Georgia's unfair laws, the Supreme Court would rule in their favor.

As the Cherokee's attorney, William Wirt, said, "what the fate of the motion will be it is impossible for any lawyer to predict with certainty; for the case is perfectly new."[1] The Cherokee case against the state of Georgia would be the first time that the United States' highest court would take up matters of Indian treaty rights. The results of the case would not only influence the fate of Native Americans but would help determine the character of the United States. The Cherokee were testing the very principles on which the United States was founded. As the Cherokee brought the legal action, they served this warning to the nation: "Our cause is your own. It is based upon your own principles, which we have learned from yourself."[2]

Attorney William Wirt was assigned to be the attorney for the Cherokee in their case against Georgia.

Chapter 1

Cherokee Land

WHEN EUROPEAN EXPLORERS first encountered them in the sixteenth century, the Cherokee occupied a sprawling territory that included much of modern-day Georgia, North and South Carolina, Tennessee, Alabama, and parts of Kentucky and Virginia. They called themselves Ani-Yunwiya; the name Cherokee was given to them by other tribes.

Agricultural Society

The Native Americans who lived in the northern and western parts of North America relied primarily on hunting for their survival. But those who settled in the southeast, which has a warm climate and long growing season, turned to agriculture for their basic needs. The Cherokee settled in clearings where they raised maize and vegetables and supplemented their diet by hunting and gathering.

Along with other southeastern tribes, they developed a highly organized civilization along the lines of the native empires of Mexico and Central America. The Cherokee built permanent villages ranging from a few hundred to several thousand residents. The people did not individually own sections of land; rather, they worked together in large fields shared by the entire community. Their political system was far more organized than that of northern tribes. Their leaders could quickly gather thousands of warriors when the need arose.

Warfare frequently broke out between the tribes of the Southeast. The Cherokee were especially at odds with the Creek and the Choctaw. Their wars, however, were not campaigns of

The Native Americans were effective farmers. They did not own individual tracts of land, but instead worked together in fields that were shared by the community.

conquest, and the disputes rarely concerned territory. Generally, they fought to avenge one or more of their members who were killed in a chance encounter with the enemy.

The Europeans Arrive

When Columbus first set foot on the shores of the Western Hemisphere in 1492, the people he mistakenly called Indians were thriving. Contact with the Europeans, however, proved disastrous for Native Americans. Many of the explorers considered them marginally human savages and killed them without remorse.

Even more devastating to the Indians were the diseases these newcomers brought. The Europeans had built up immunities over the centuries to many of the deadliest microorganisms in their environment. The immune systems of the Native Americans, however, were totally unprepared for the germs that came ashore from the sailing ships. Diseases such as smallpox and measles roared through Native American populations like fire through a parched forest.

By the time Europeans began settling along the Atlantic coastline of North America in the late sixteenth and early seventeenth centuries, many of the original inhabitants of the land had disappeared. Historians estimate that over 90 percent of the Native Americans were swept away in the great epidemics brought by Europeans. Like other tribes, the Cherokee had faded to only a shadow of their former influence when Great Britain began establishing colonies on the fringes of their territory.

The British justified their settlements on this new territory through a European interpretation of international law known as the right of discovery. Under this concept, Christian European nations claimed the right to settle and administer lands occupied

When the British discovered new lands, they would appropriate them for their country. All Native Americans were considered to be inferior because of their ignorance of Christianity and their lack of "civilization."

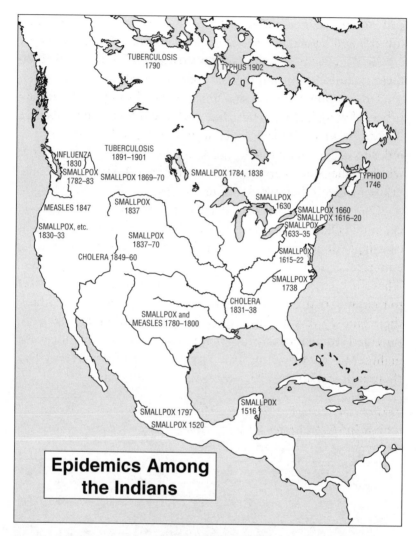

TUBERCULOSIS 1790

TYPHUS 1902

INFLUENZA 1830

TUBERCULOSIS 1891–1901

SMALLPOX 1782–83

SMALLPOX 1869–70

SMALLPOX 1784, 1838

TYPHOID 1746

MEASLES 1847

SMALLPOX 1837

SMALLPOX 1630

SMALLPOX 1660
SMALLPOX 1616–20
SMALLPOX 1633–35

SMALLPOX, etc. 1830–33

SMALLPOX 1837–70

SMALLPOX 1615–22

CHOLERA 1849–60

SMALLPOX 1738

SMALLPOX and MEASLES 1780–1800

CHOLERA 1831–38

SMALLPOX 1797
SMALLPOX 1520

SMALLPOX 1516

Epidemics Among the Indians

by "uncivilized," non-Christian people who were judged to be incapable of understanding "civilized" definitions of ownership. Whichever European country "discovered" the land gained title to it and had the right to occupy it.

Lifestyle Upheaval

The Europeans were fascinated by the abundance of wildlife in North America, particularly furbearing animals such as beaver whose hides could be used for clothing. Early traders offered Native Americans a variety of manufactured goods such as cooking utensils and hatchets in exchange for these furs. Gradually, many Native Americans came to change their way of life and relied on these manufactured goods instead of their traditional materials.

Unscrupulous traders also introduced whiskey to the Indian tribes. Having had no experience with the intoxicating effects of this drink, many Indians' lives were destroyed by addiction. In order to ensure a steady flow of the goods they needed and the whiskey that some craved, Native Americans had to spend more of their time and energy hunting.

Over the course of a few generations, tribes whose economies had been primarily based on agriculture became increasingly dependent on hunting. The most precious furbearing animals lived in colder climates than the Cherokee occupied. Therefore, they did not get caught up in this cultural upheaval to the same extreme as northern tribes. They continued to farm their lands. Nevertheless, the European market for deerskin provided strong incentive for them to hunt. By the middle of the eighteenth century, the Cherokee were trading twenty-five thousand deerskins a year for manufactured goods.

The items that Europeans bartered with the Native Americans sometimes had devastating effects. Alcohol, for example, ruined the lives of many Native Americans.

The demand for furs and skins eventually took its toll on animal populations. Before long, Indians had to range farther and farther from home to collect the pelts they needed to obtain desired manufactured goods. This put stress on the traditional, stationary farm life of the Cherokee. It also forced them to range outside of their traditional hunting grounds, putting them into conflict with unfriendly tribes. These enemies, in turn, ranged into Cherokee lands in search of increasingly scarce game. The small skirmishes on the fringes of tribal territory flared up into almost constant warfare.

At the same time, the two European nations competing for the resources of eastern North America, France and Great Britain, recruited Indian allies to help their causes. Conflicts between hunting parties and hostilities between the French and English and their allies combined to plunge Indian tribes into relentless warfare. This reached its peak in the bloody French and Indian War, fought from 1754 to 1763.

Setting Boundaries

The British defeat of the French in the French and Indian War settled the question of which nation would control eastern North America. But the war did nothing to extinguish the smoldering bitterness between various Indian tribes and groups of European settlers.

Much of this conflict arose from the clash of cultures regarding ownership of the land. As was customary among Native Americans, the Cherokee did not accept the concept that individuals could own plots of land. But they did claim a vast territory which all of their people had the right to use as they saw fit. They grew increasingly resentful of the thousands of British colonists who edged farther and farther into their lands. In the settlers' minds, the Cherokee were just another group of uncivilized savages whose land was there for the taking. By the right of discovery and later treaties with France, all of eastern North America belonged to Great Britain. Therefore, the British believed they could settle wherever they wished.

At the end of the French and Indian War, the British government tried to prevent hostilities that might arise from the chaotic jumble of land claims by settlers and the vaguely defined territory

THE FRENCH AND INDIAN WAR

Although most of the fighting in the French and Indian War occurred far from Cherokee territory, it was a conflict that sealed the fate of the Indians. The war began as a border dispute near what is now Pittsburgh, Pennsylvania, between French Canadians and British Americans in 1754. The home nations of both colonies sent regular troops to North America the following year to protect their interests. After frequent clashes between the two forces, the two nations formally declared war. The bad feelings between France and Great Britain spilled over into Europe, where the two nations became engaged in the Seven Years' War.

The French and their Indian allies held the upper hand through much of the early fighting. It was in two early defeats that George Washington, a young officer in the Virginia militia, learned some practical lessons in the art of wilderness warfare. But eventually the French government lost enthusiasm for the conflict, while the British government pressed on in its determination. The poorly supported French troops lost the key Canadian cities of Quebec and Montreal by 1760, which, for all practical purposes, determined the war's outcome. From that time until the American Revolution, Great Britain and not France would dominate the North American continent.

This proved disastrous for Native Americans. The French government had maintained colonies that sought to live with or alongside the Indians. Although the French Canadians sought to convert Indians to Christianity, they generally showed more respect for Indian culture than did the British. The British government was never able to enforce its established boundaries between its colonists and the Native Americans. After winning their independence from Great Britain, those colonists continued their aggressive expansion, which destroyed the Indian cultures.

To prevent land claim disputes, a peace treaty was written which established the boundary line between Indian lands and British colonial settlements.

claims of the Native Americans. In 1763, the peace settlement with the French and Indian tribes decreed an official boundary line between Indian lands and British colonial settlements. The line ran down from Canada through western New England and Pennsylvania and along the Appalachian Mountains to the South. According to British design, anything west of the line would remain Indian land, while anything east was available to settlers.

The boundary cut through some of the territory traditionally claimed by the Cherokee. But since most of their lands lay to the west and because they feared losing even more land as punishment for some of their members fighting against the British, the Cherokee gave up their claim to most of their lands east of the boundary.

Legacy of Bitterness

The Proclamation of 1763 upset many colonists who saw no reason why they should let the claims of savages stand in the way of civilization. Many of them ignored the official boundary and began establishing settlements in Kentucky and eastern Tennessee. Recognizing the trouble they would have throwing settlers off such lands, the British altered the boundary somewhat in 1768. In exchange for allowing the Cherokee to reserve a bit more of their land in Georgia, the British opened up Kentucky and eastern Tennessee to settlers.

Restless pioneers, however, paid no more attention to the new boundaries than to the old ones. The Cherokee were continually irritated by whites setting up claims on the eastern fringes of their traditional land. Confrontations between Native Americans and settlers occasionally ended in bloodshed, which provoked more cycles of vengeful violence. Historian Anthony F. C. Wallace writes, "A legacy of bitterness over atrocities on both sides remained for generations, Western frontiersmen condemning the Indians as murdering savages and the Indians despising the Americans as untrustworthy and brutal."[3]

The Americans Take Control

The Cherokee's anger at the colonists led them to side with the British during the American Revolution. Given past experience, it was easy for British agents to persuade the Cherokee that their territory claims would be respected only if the British kept control.

The fighting went badly for the Cherokee, however. The militia from the neighboring southern states went after Indian villages as well as armies. After suffering heavy losses, the Cherokee agreed to a peace treaty on May 20, 1777, in which they gave up their claim to some eastern lands. But individual settlers and Cherokee continued to resort to violence to settle their personal disputes. Before the war ended, problems between the Cherokee and colonists escalated into more warfare. Near the end of the Revolution, the colonists launched a military campaign against the Cherokee that burned more than fifty of their towns and destroyed their crops and livestock.

The war strengthened the Americans' claims on Indian land. Along with the right of discovery, the settlers argued that they had conquered the Indians in war. Just as defeat had cost the British their rights to North America, their Indian allies had lost their rights to the land. By this time, warfare and disease had slashed the remaining Cherokee population of thirty thousand

The Cherokee, growing weary of the white settler's encroachment on their lands, fought back. The war resulted in the destruction of many of their towns and crops.

nearly in half. Like many of the badly outnumbered Native American tribes, they had little choice but to agree to unfavorable terms.

The success of the United States in achieving independence further complicated the land disputes. In the 1783 peace agreement that ended the American Revolution, Great Britain surrendered to the United States all of its claims to land under the right of discovery. But nowhere did the agreement mention anything about Indian territorial claims. The new nation was still in the process of determining how to govern itself, and therefore many different groups took it upon themselves to resolve questions of Indian land claims. Instead of dealing with a single nation—Great Britain—the Cherokee found themselves trying to settle land disputes with thirteen separate state governments, a new federal government whose powers were still being debated, and renegade pioneers who took matters into their own hands.

Who's in Charge?

As the federal and state governments wrestled for authority, U.S.-Indian relations became a confused and often contradictory mess. State governments, particularly in the South, became very aggressive in dealing with Indian territory. They argued that Great Britain had surrendered all of its territorial claims to the individual states, not to the federal government. North Carolina, for example, granted a large section of Cherokee land in Tennessee to its citizens in 1783. From 1784 to 1789, various local and state governments signed treaties with Native Americans who gave up rights to territory. Many of these Indians had no authority from their people to do so. Frequently, no interpreters were present; the Indians had no clear idea of what they were signing.

Meanwhile, federal agents were trying to negotiate agreements with Indians on behalf of the entire nation. As early as 1775, before the fighting began in the American Revolution, the Continental Congress divided the country into departments and appointed commissioners to set Indian policy within those departments. In 1778, the newly declared United States signed its first treaty with Indian peoples. Following the Revolutionary

FEDERAL TREATIES

The Cherokee tribe cited several federal treaties in arguing their right to self-government on their land. The most important of these was the Treaty of Hopewell, signed at Hopewell, South Carolina, on November 28, 1785. This treaty was the first general treaty with Native Americans ever signed by the newly formed government of the United States. It established definite boundaries between the United States and the Cherokee Nation. At the same time, the Cherokee Nation acknowledged U.S. control over issues such as the tribe's right to trade with foreign nations. The following January, the Choctaw and Chickasaw tribes signed a similar agreement at Hopewell.

White settlers, however, consistently violated the treaty. The Cherokee called upon the U.S. government to enforce the Treaty of Hopewell. When it was not able or willing to do so, the Cherokee began to fight back. The federal government settled the conflict with the Treaty of Holston, signed on July 2, 1791. In this treaty, the Cherokee gave up lands they had already lost to white settlers in exchange for a clearly stated promise that the U.S. government would, in the future, guarantee the Cherokee possession of their remaining land.

The Northwest Ordinance did not directly involve the Cherokee. It was a law that Congress passed on July 13, 1787, at the urging of real estate speculators who wanted to set up colonies in the lands north of the Ohio River. Article 3 of the ordinance stated: "The utmost good faith shall always be observed towards the Indians; their lands and property shall never be taken from them without their consent; and, in their property, rights, and liberty, they shall never be invaded or disturbed; unless in just and lawful wars authorized by Congress; but laws founded in justice and humanity shall from time to time be made for preventing wrongs being done to them."

The Cherokee believed that this statement expressed the intent of Congress in the federal government's dealings with Native Americans.

War, in 1785, federal commissioners signed the Treaty of Hopewell. This agreement defined the borders of the United States and the Cherokee people and recognized the right of the Cherokee to their territory.

Conquered People or Foreign Nations?

As shown by the language of the Treaty of Hopewell, the federal government was in the process of rethinking the theory that the

United States held title to all Indian land by virtue of conquering them in the American Revolution. The fierce resistance of Native Americans against efforts to drive them from their land had proved how faulty this notion was. According to several scholars, the decision to abandon the claim of conquest "reflected the reality that native military power could be neither ignored nor countered without an enormous investment in lives and money."[4] In its dealings with Native Americans, the federal government returned to the old British colonial policy. It conceded that the Indians had ownership rights to their traditional lands. The right of discovery that Great Britain had given to the United States meant only that the United States had the sole right to purchase the lands *if* the Indians chose to sell.

The Northwest Ordinance of 1787, enacted by Congress, specifically stated that Indian "land and property shall never be taken from them without their consent."[5] Three years later, Congress passed a law declaring that the only legal sales of Indian land were those that resulted from a public treaty with the federal government.

The federal government continued to have a strong interest in acquiring Indian lands. For one thing, it had no money with which to pay the thousands of soldiers who had fought in the Revolution. The easiest solution to this problem was to pay off the soldiers with land. Much of the land in Indian territory was unoccupied and therefore a tempting target for settlement. But rather than simply seizing Indian lands, the U.S. Constitution authorized the federal government to take what many Americans were coming to see as a more honorable course of action—negotiating treaties for the purchase of those lands. Negotiations with Indians proceeded much as they would with any foreign country.

The Federal Government Takes Over

States such as North Carolina and Georgia protested that the federal government had no power to get involved in matters concerning state territory. But the U.S. Congress took the position that territorial disputes between settlers and Indians posed a real threat of war to the nation. In matters of national security, the

FIVE CIVILIZED TRIBES

When the English began to make forays into the interior of southeastern North America, they discovered cultures so organized and well-developed that some of the explorers believed the Indians were the remnant of the Ten Lost Tribes of Israel. The five principal tribes of the area, the Creek, Cherokee, Choctaw, Chickasaw, and Seminole, lived in permanent settlements, grew crops, and showed interest and ability in adapting to white culture. This led whites to refer to them as the "Five Civilized Tribes."

During the early days of white settlement, the largest and most influential of these tribes was the Creek, whose domain extended from Georgia to Alabama. The Creek tribe, however, split into two factions over whether to make war on the Americans, who were crowding into their territory in the early 1800s. The more aggressive group, known as the Red Sticks, were decimated by the Creek War in which their traditional enemies, the Cherokee, fought alongside the United States. After the war, the Cherokee replaced the Creek as the dominant southern tribe.

This document shows the seals of the "Five Civilized Tribes."

The Choctaw lived to the west of the Creek, and the Chickasaw ranged on the Creek's northwest borders. Neither group was as united as either the Creek or Cherokee tribes, and both disintegrated as distinct nations during many years of fighting and relocation. The Seminole, who were closely allied with the Creek, occupied southern Georgia and parts of Florida. A group of Seminole under Osceola retreated into the swamps of Florida, where they were able to resist efforts to drive them out longer than any other eastern Native American tribe.

federal government had the authority to act on behalf of all the states. Furthermore, the newly approved Constitution gave the federal government the power to regulate commerce with Indian tribes. In 1793, Congress strengthened its control over Indian matters by passing a law banning the sale of all Indian land unless the sale was part of a treaty signed by the federal government.

Eventually, even the southern states grudgingly conceded that the federal government would be responsible for handling Indian matters. Georgia, for example, had long insisted that the king of England had granted the state a vast tract of land that included large sections of territory claimed by the Cherokee and Creek. In the 1790s, some state officials sold large sections of this land, in what is now Alabama and Mississippi, to investors. When these transactions came to light, the federal government declared them illegal because only the U.S. government was authorized to deal with Indian land. The result was a financial catastrophe. Many investors had paid their life's savings for land that was not theirs. Many of those who sold the land were either bankrupt or had run off, so the investors could not get their money back.

To clear up the mess, the United States and Georgia made a deal in 1802. Georgia agreed to cede, or give up, its claim to Alabama and Mississippi to the federal government. The state also left it to the federal government to deal with the Cherokee who continued to live and claim land within Georgia's boundaries. In exchange, the United States agreed to pay Georgia for the land it had ceded and promised to buy all Indian lands within the remaining boundary of Georgia as soon as possible.

Promises, Promises

Promises from the federal government were one thing. Honoring those promises in the face of opposition from both settlers and Indians proved to be quite another. Thousands of settlers eager for new land flowed into territory claimed by Native Americans. Federal officials were ashamed at this blatant violation of the Treaty of Hopewell. But with little money, no standing army, and no tradition of authority, the federal government could not force those illegally occupying land to leave. The best the United States could do was try to negotiate new treaties, pay the Indians for the land that the settlers had illegally taken, and take stronger measures to prohibit further movement into Indian territory.

This strategy ran into difficulties because Native Americans resisted efforts of the United States to buy their land. Most agreed with a Creek leader who declared, "We would not receive money for land in which our fathers and friends are buried." [6]

Pressure from settlers illegally crowding them off land, from states trying to impose their own will, and from the United States hounding them to accept money in exchange for territory occasionally caused Native Americans to fight back. Several tribes joined forces in the north to fight the United States; most of the southern tribes, including the Cherokee, fought independently in brief skirmishes from the mid-1780s to the mid-1790s. The northern wars officially ended with the signing of the Treaty of Greenville in 1795. In this agreement, the United States promised to take on the responsibility of guaranteeing that all Indians would be dealt with fairly and honorably in the future.

The Cherokee Try to Fit In

Such guarantees by the federal government, combined with the hopelessness of trying to fight a people who outnumbered them so badly, led the Cherokee to abandon warfare. After 1795, the Cherokee tried

This advertisement urges whites to buy land in the Indian territories.

to settle all disputes with the United States through peaceful means. Rather than taking up arms when settlers trespassed on their land, they appealed to the U.S. government to uphold its promises.

The Cherokee also decided that the best way to ensure their survival in the middle of this growing, hostile American society, was to accept the ways of the whites. More than any other Native American people, the Cherokee adopted the culture of the whites. As a demonstration of their determination to live in peace with their European neighbors, they joined the American forces as allies against the Creek in 1813. Their heroic efforts were a decisive factor in the defeat of the Creek at Horseshoe Bend, Alabama, the battle that finally settled the Creek War. In that conflict, a Cherokee warrior named Junaluska reportedly saved the life of the U.S. commander, Andrew Jackson.

The Cherokee's hopes that their cooperation would be rewarded, however, were to be dashed repeatedly.

Chapter 2

Federal Policy: Civilize or Relocate?

CHIEF JUSTICE JOHN Marshall once observed, "The condition of the Indians in relation to the United States is perhaps unlike that of any other two people in existence."[7] The European explorers' policy of claiming and colonizing land that was already occupied created an awkward situation. Many U.S. citizens felt guilty about pushing the Native Americans off their land and nearly annihilating their populations. They recognized the Indians' right to live where they had lived for centuries. Yet there was no practical way to turn back the clock and make things right. White settlers were well established, cities were thriving, and pioneers were champing at the bit to move into more sparsely populated Indian territory.

This left the United States with large pockets of unconquered and independent people within its declared borders. No established tradition in European law governed such a unique situation. Early leaders of the United States had to invent policy as they went along, and they ended up promoting two policies that were directly contradictory.

Knox and Indian Assimilation

The most important government official in the formation of federal Indian policy was Henry Knox. Knox served as the nation's first secretary of war in the administration of George Washington. Like many Americans, Knox was somewhat ashamed of the

Secretary of war Henry Knox was appalled by the persecution of Native Americans. He expressed his disapproval for the conquered nation approach, believing that Indians should be treated as if they were citizens of a foreign nation.

way whites had treated and were continuing to treat the Indians. He was alarmed at the racist attitudes of many frontier settlers who seemed determined to exterminate Native Americans. Unlike these settlers, Knox did not believe that Indians were naturally inferior to whites.

It was Knox who urged Washington to abandon the conquered nation approach and instead have the federal government deal with Native Americans through treaties, just as they would with foreign nations. He viewed this policy as beneficial to both sides— it would protect the Indians from almost certain extinction, and it would help the United States avoid costly wars with Native Americans at a time when the nation was desperate for money.

Knox realized that treaties alone would not prevent the Indians from being overwhelmed by American settlers. Indian and European-based cultures were so different that there would inevitably be conflict wherever they met. In any clash of cultures, the one with greater numbers prevails in the end. Knox saw two solutions to this problem. One was to prevent conflicts by purchasing land from Native Americans and directing their peaceful removal from that land before opening it up to whites for settlement. Every president from George Washington to John Quincy Adams followed this course of action.

HENRY KNOX

Few colonists did as much as Henry Knox to aid the American Revolution, and yet few people other than historians have ever heard of him. Knox was born in 1750, the seventh of ten sons in his family. At the age of twelve, he began working for a bookseller in Boston, and in 1771 he opened his own bookstore in the city.

At the beginning of the fighting in the Revolution, he rose quickly to the rank of colonel in an artillery unit. Unfortunately, the Continental Army had virtually no artillery of its own. The American leadership assigned him to get fifty-five cannon from the recently captured British Fort Ticonderoga in northern New York. Knox did a masterful job of supervising the hauling of these heavy guns three hundred miles across ice and snow. When they arrived in Boston, the cannon forced the British army to evacuate the city.

His artillery was crucial in many of the battles of the Continental Army, and Knox earned the trust and friendship of General George Washington. He rose to the army's highest rank of major general, and at the end of the war he was called upon to replace Washington as commander of the army.

Knox believed in a strong federal government. During the formation of the nation's government in the 1780s, he accepted the post of secretary of war. After the Constitution was adopted and Washington elected president in 1789, Knox stayed on as the nation's first secretary of war (an office that later came to be known as secretary of defense). In addition to his formation of Indian policy, his most noteworthy accomplishment during his six years as secretary of war was the quick defeat of Shays's Rebellion, an uprising of disgruntled farmers in Massachussetts.

This strategy, however, worked only when Indians were willing to sell their territory. Tribes such as the Cherokee increasingly resisted U.S. offers to purchase land. In such cases, Knox believed that the only way for Indians to survive among the growing white population was to become "civilized," by which he meant living a lifestyle similar to that of the whites. For, while he did not believe Indians to be inferior, he did believe their culture was inferior. Knox urged both the federal government and private individuals to take an active role in helping the Indians to adopt white culture. His initiative eventually led Congress to create a Civilization Fund, the purpose of which was to support Indian education.

"Instead of exterminating a part of the human race," declared Knox, the United States should transfer "our knowledge of cultivation and the arts to the aboriginals of the country."[8] He spoke of instilling Indians with a desire to own their own property, in the belief that land disputes between Indians and whites would be reduced if the two sides held the same attitudes and beliefs about private ownership of land.

Indian Reform

The attempt to "civilize" Native Americans became known as the Indian reform movement, and it was popular primarily in the Northeast. Its goal was perhaps best expressed by Congregational minister Jedidiah Morse who said that Native Americans, particularly the southern tribes, could be "educated where they are and raised to the rank and privilege of citizens, and merged in the mass of the nation."[9] Among those who spoke out in favor of Indian reform was Thomas Jefferson. Upon assuming the office of president in 1801, Jefferson told the nation of his hopes for the Indians. "In leading them . . . to agriculture, to manufacturing activities, and civilization; in bringing together their and our sentiments, and in preparing them ultimately to participate in the benefits of our Government, I trust and believe we are acting for their greatest good."[10]

Supporters of Indian reform, both in the government and in religious mission groups, set about providing the materials and

One of many reformers trying to assimilate the Native Americans into white culture and Christianity, this missionary tries to convert the Indians from their religious beliefs.

the training for Indians to adopt white culture. Around the turn of the nineteenth century, Indian tribes were being taught the use of European farm implements, and they learned trades such as blacksmithing and operating mills and other heavy machinery. Reformers also sought to teach reading, writing, and European music and arts to Indian tribes.

The Cherokee and Reform

Following the disastrous wars of the late eighteenth century, the Cherokee asked the advice of important American leaders as to how they could preserve their tribe and their homeland from encroaching settlers. Jefferson was among those who advised them to take up the reformers' goal of assimilation.

Adapting to white culture was not as difficult for the Cherokee as it was for northern and plains tribes. Although whites tended to think of all Native Americans as nomadic hunters who needed to be taught to settle down and farm the land, the Cherokee had traditionally been a farming people. Like their white neighbors, they had always lived in permanent villages. In many ways they were already living lifestyles similar to the whites. Furthermore, they did not recognize a great gulf between the races. They saw nothing wrong with accepting whites into their society. Intermarriage was not considered shocking, and the Cherokee Nation included many people of mixed race who had access to white culture.

The Cherokee eagerly set about to learn other parts of white culture that they saw could be useful. Some of them copied the clothing styles of their white neighbors. Like their white counterparts in the South, they planted large fields of cotton and purchased African slaves to work them. Cherokee people became shop owners, business owners, and craftspeople. They welcomed the mission societies that helped them set up schools. Before long, Cherokee villages looked much like those of their neighbors.

Opposition to Reform

Unfortunately for the Cherokee, the United States was pursuing a second national Indian policy at the same time. In opposition to the reformers were large numbers of westerners and southerners who did not relish the idea of living among Indians. The bitter clashes along the frontier in the previous generation had left them distrustful of Native Americans. These citizens regarded Indians as a constant menace and suspected them of plotting with foreign powers to overthrow the U.S. government. They never surrendered the notion that the Indians were an inferior, conquered people whose land belonged to the United States.

To these people, the idea of civilizing Indians was absurd. Senator John Forsyth of Georgia expressed their point of view when he called the Indians, "a race not admitted to be equal to the rest of the community, treated somewhat like human beings; . . . not yet entitled and probably never will be entitled, to equal civil and political rights." [11] People like Forsyth wanted the Indians cleared out of the way so that whites could use the land.

Support for removal was found even among those who were sympathetic to Indians. A large number of Americans held the view that the United States was a special gift from God. They believed, as their pioneer ancestors had, that God had set aside

John Forsyth of Georgia, who advocated driving Indians off of their lands.

this new land for his faithful people. While they had no personal quarrel with Indians, they could not see that non-Christians had any place in God's bold new nation. They assumed that Indians could never adapt to white ways, and that they would want to sell their lands and retreat into the western wilderness as civilization surrounded them. When Indians instead clung to their lands despite suffering at the hands of hostile settlers, Americans decided that Native Americans needed to be removed by the government for their own good.

In the early nineteenth century, southern whites had yet another reason to want Indians out of the way. The expansion of the British Empire into Asia had opened up vast new markets for cotton goods produced by British factories. In order to meet the demand, the British were buying up all the American cotton they could find and paying top dollar for it. American factories in the Northeast tried to compete with the British, adding to the demand. Profits for cotton farmers grew so lucrative that even a moderate-sized field of average-quality cotton could produce a fortune.

Southern farmers, hoping to cash in on the situation, abandoned their worn-out cotton fields and looked for more land on which to establish new fields. But the expanding population had already bought up most of the good farmland. Prospective cotton farmers cast jealous eyes on Indian territory, most of which they saw as unoccupied wilderness. They put pressure on lawmakers to open up such land for white farmers. Some farmers ignored the laws and the established boundaries and began clearing tribal land for themselves. In such an environment, a second U.S. Indian policy gathered strength—the removal of the Indians.

Indian Removal

Ironically, Thomas Jefferson, who spoke so eloquently of enfolding Native Americans into U.S. society, lit the fuse on this explosive policy. Less than two years after his speech in support of civilizing Indians, Jefferson proposed a policy that sabotaged it. He had come to doubt that Indians could prosper among the hordes of white settlers pressing for their land. Furthermore, he was concerned about how to defend the remote western borders of his country against foreign nations such as Spain and France. His purchase of the sprawling Louisiana Territory in 1803 gave him an idea for solving both problems. Perhaps both whites and Indians would be better off if all Native Americans moved into these new lands west of the Mississippi. The Indians could have their own space where they could have time to adopt the ways of European-style civilization. At the same time, they could provide a buffer zone against enemies while the growing white settlements expanded the U.S. power base in the East.

Jefferson tried to persuade lawmakers to pass a constitutional amendment to provide for the transfer of all eastern Indians to this new territory. Congress, however, was too cautious to join in such a radical scheme. Jefferson then tried to convince tribes such as the Chickasaw that they would be better off selling their lands and moving west. "Instead of inviting Indians to come within our limits, our objective is to tempt them to evacuate them,"[12] he said. When they balked, Jefferson became so impatient that he urged federal agents to use underhanded tactics to get the Indians to move. He advised them to see to it that "the good and influential individuals run into debt"[13] because that would force the Indians to sell their lands in order to pay off the debts.

Voluntary Removal

Despite bewilderment over Jefferson's conflicting advice, the Cherokee seriously considered his removal suggestion. Many of

JEFFERSON'S PUZZLING CONTRADICTIONS

Historians agree that Thomas Jefferson was one of the most intelligent and resourceful leaders in U.S. history. He was blessed with a gift for eloquently expressing the highest principles of human behavior. Yet his actions frequently failed to live up to his beautifully expressed philosophy. The writer of the Declaration of Independence, who boldly declared that "all men are created equal," owned slaves all of his life. The passionate defender of free speech tried to imprison political rivals for criticizing his presidential policies.

The contradiction between words and actions was never more obvious than in his policies toward Native Americans. Jefferson had genuinely liked and admired Indians ever since his childhood, when friendly neighboring Cherokee occasionally visited his family. He studied Indians carefully and collected vocabularies for more than fifty dialects—probably the largest collection of its kind at that time. Jefferson considered Indians the intellectual equal of whites, and he cited their speeches as proof. Indian leaders, he said, "astonish you with strokes of the most sublime oratory . . . their images glowing and elevated." In his view, Indians lived more primitively than whites only because of their environment and low population.

In the early years of his presidency, Jefferson became concerned that the spread of white settlers was unstoppable and that it would eventually engulf and destroy the Native American tribes. The compassionate solution, then, was to buy time for the Indians by moving them to the west, where they could gradually adopt the ways of the whites.

But as often happened, Jefferson got bogged down in the question of how to get people to do what was, in his opinion, in the nation's best interest, and stop doing what was against it. So convinced was Jefferson that removal was in the best interests of Native Americans that he became willing to sacrifice their freedom of self-determination to achieve it. Although his motives were good, he ended up initiating the federal removal policy that so devastated the southeastern tribes.

them had gone through too many bad experiences with whites to believe that the United States would accept Indians who adopted their culture. They wondered if they would be better off starting over in a place where whites did not constantly harrass them.

In 1809, a delegation of Cherokee men traveled west to scout the lands that the federal government was promoting for their use. Based on their report, a sizable part of the Cherokee Nation was at least willing to consider seriously the idea of removal. In fact, the prospect was attractive enough to entice about a third of the Cherokee to move into the present-day Oklahoma from 1817 to 1819.

The result was, for the most part, a disaster. Emigrants found themselves under attack from hostile whites and Indians alike. In addition they suffered from diseases, and were unable to raise the food they needed to survive. As one Indian agent described the situation, "the five hundred Cherokees who reached here this year have been forced to sell their claims on the government for provisions to relieve their suffering." [14]

Blind to the harsh realities of the situation, U.S. leaders continued to come up with schemes for removing Indians from white population areas. In the early 1820s, President James Monroe and his secretary of war, John Calhoun, pushed voluntary removal plans as the best solution for Indians. Lewis Cass, a prominent politician who governed the Michigan Territory for eighteen years and eventually ran for president on the Democratic ticket in 1848, kept alive the notion that Indians were savages incapable of civilization and so must be removed.

In 1823, Senator John Forsyth of Georgia proposed setting aside a huge reservation east of the Mississippi River. The U.S. government would give a plot of land to each family, which was guaranteed to remain theirs until 1900, at which time all Indians would become U.S. citizens. While Congress would oversee the reservation's operation, the Indians would be allowed to elect their own assembly.

Determined to Stay

The Indian removal proposals in the 1820s were largely unsuccessful. After learning the fate of their people, the remaining

Cherokee in the East were dead set against removal. In 1823, they declared, "It is the fixed and unalterable determination of this nation never again to cede one foot more of our land."[15] The tribe turned its back on removal and focused all of its energy on the alternative solution of assimilation, with one important exception. Unlike the whites' system of individual ownership of land, all title to Cherokee lands belonged to the Cherokee Nation. No one in the tribe could sell any of this land without the approval of the Cherokee government.

Seeing the value of reading and writing, the Cherokee decided to make use of these skills in their own language. In the 1820s, an inventive Cherokee named Sequoyah devised an alphabet for the Cherokee language. A year later, the tribe set up its own printing press. Shortly thereafter, Elias Boudinot printed his first issue of the first Native American newspaper, the *Cherokee Phoenix*.

Many Cherokee accepted and began to practice the Christian religion. Some of their members became wealthy planters and showed they could operate businesses better than many whites.

The Cherokee admired the U.S. system of government and patterned their own government after it. They set up their own house of representatives and senate to enact laws as well as a system of courts to handle their legal disputes. They built a capital city, known as New Echota, in their Georgia territory.

On July 26, 1827, the Cherokee Nation adopted its own constitution, in accordance with established European legal traditions. Having done so much to follow Jefferson's advice that they adapt to white culture, they hoped that the whites would see them as good and peaceful neighbors.

Unfortunately, the Cherokee's success in following Jefferson's advice to assimilate backfired on them. Many of them became so successful that jealous whites demanded to know why the government let 'savage Indians' own so much land and property while poor whites had to struggle just to put food on the table. Georgians were particularly incensed at the Cherokee's constitution, in which they declared themselves to be an independent, self-governing nation. Georgia politicians scoffed at

SEQUOYAH AND THE WRITTEN LANGUAGE

One of the most remarkable accomplishments of the Cherokee in their quest to absorb white culture was the development of a written language by Sequoyah. Sequoyah was born around 1770 to a Cherokee woman, Wureth. His father is widely believed to have been an American trader, Nathaniel Gist. He went by a series of names: he named himself George Guess, but the Cherokee called him Sogwali, and British missionaries called him Sequoyah, the name he is best known by today.

Sequoyah.

Although he worked as a silversmith, his most exceptional skill was in languages. He became intrigued with what many Indians called "talking leaves," the written language of the whites. He wondered if some of the whites' power had to do with their mastery of writing.

In 1809, he set about to create a written form for the Cherokee language. His first approach was to create a different picture for each Cherokee word, but he quickly realized this would be too unwieldy. He saw that he would be better off creating a symbol for each sound in the language rather than a symbol for each word. He began creating a syllabary, whose letters stood for the syllables that made up Cherokee words.

The work was difficult, and Sequoyah built himself a cabin where he could work undisturbed. This upset his wife, who at one point stormed into the cabin and threw all his papers in the fireplace. But with the help of his daughter, he adapted letters from Greek, Hebrew, and English to invent a written form of the Cherokee language. His alphabet contained eighty-five characters, one for each sound used in their speech.

In 1821, the Cherokee Council approved the use of Sequoyah's written language. Within a few years, many Cherokee were able to read and write in this form. Elias Boudinot used Sequoyah's language in publishing the *Cherokee Phoenix*.

Sequoyah moved to Arkansas in 1823 to spread his written language among Cherokee living in the west. He moved to Indian Territory (Oklahoma) five years later, where his syllabary became widely used by transplanted Cherokee living there. He died in 1843 in Mexico.

the Cherokee, comparing them to children playing with a pretend government. Whether they liked it or not, the Cherokee lived in the state of Georgia, and Georgia was not going to tolerate any independent governments within its borders.

Georgia Waits Impatiently

The Cherokee had the misfortune of claiming a homeland that happened to fall within the borders of a hotbed of Indian removal advocacy. Theda Perdue and Michael Green, editors of *The Cherokee Removal*, write, "No state agitated more consistently or aggressively for the expulsion of Native people from within its borders, no legislature sent more resolutions to Congress, no congressional delegation worked harder, and no press devoted more space to its support."[16]

The Georgians were particularly upset that the federal government had allowed the Cherokee to retain ownership of land within the borders of Georgia. They thought they had solved that problem with the agreement of 1802, in which the United States promised to buy up all remaining Indian lands in the state. But Georgians had waited more than twenty years, and there was no sign that the federal government was making any progress in living up to that promise.

As demand for land became frantic, Georgians fumed at the situation. They noted that in the years since they had signed that agreement with the United States, all other states in the Union had managed to remove virtually their entire Indian populations. "While Indians have receded thousands of miles before civilization and population in other states of the Union," declared one of Georgia's U.S. representatives, Wilson Lumpkin, "the frontier of Georgia has comparatively remained stationary."[17] Why should Georgia be singled out as the one state obligated to allow an independent Indian nation within its borders?

The federal government insisted that it was doing all it could. In 1820, President Monroe requested money from Congress to buy all Indian lands in Georgia. But the Cherokee refused to sell. In 1823, the frustration of Georgia's citizens neared the boiling point. The state asked Monroe to remove the Cherokee by force.

Monroe declined, saying that the United States was bound by treaties of 1785 and 1806 in which it had recognized Cherokee ownership of their lands in Georgia. Furthermore, the United States was on record in other treaties as promising that the Indians would not be forced off their lands. If the Cherokee chose not to sell, there was nothing the federal government could do.

Andrew Jackson Tilts the Balance

Angry Georgians began speaking of taking matters into their own hands. In 1825, federal agents won some land concessions from the Creek tribe on behalf of Georgia. The state immediately began to survey the land. Suspecting fraud on the part of the U.S. negotiators, President John Quincy Adams tried to halt the surveying. This was too much for the governor of Georgia, who ordered citizens of the state to prepare for battle against the federal government. Adams backed away from his stand.

Encouraged by this success, Georgians sought ways to get rid of the Indians and see to it that every square inch of Georgia belonged solely to Georgia. Their prospects for success brightened greatly with the election of Andrew Jackson as president. A product of the western frontier, Jackson had long been on record in opposition to Indian treaty rights. As far as he was concerned, they had none. He regarded Indians as unfortunate savages who

James Monroe (top)
Andrew Jackson (bottom).

should not be allowed to stand in the way of U.S. expansion. During his days as a federal Indian commissioner, he had secretly and illegally surveyed Indian lands and, without approval from superiors, made shady treaty agreements that earned him a tidy personal fortune. As a general, he had refused orders to remove settlers from lands they had illegally occupied.

Jackson thought negotiating treaties with Indians was ridiculous. Notes historian Harry L. Watson, "Though Jackson himself had negotiated many Indian treaties, he had done so in bad faith, privately believing that Congress and the states had the right to seize all Indian lands at pleasure." [18] The United States, Jackson believed, had conquered the Indians and, being far stronger than they were, should just take whatever it wanted from them.

Jackson certainly did not believe the federal government had to recognize any Indian claim to own land within the boundaries of a state. According to Jackson, that violated the Constitution by interfering with the states' right to self-government. What government in the world would allow a people to set up their own nation within its borders, he wanted to know?

Jackson insisted he did not hate Indians; in fact, he claimed sympathy for them. But he believed that the federal government could not interfere with the affairs of a state. Because it could not protect the Indians, removal and relocation were the only way to save them from bloody annihilation. He claimed that he had a moral duty to carry out relocation to protect the Indians from destruction at the hands of white settlers.

Perdue and Green observe, "Andrew Jackson won election to the presidency in 1828 with almost unanimous support from southern voters, who believed he would expel the Indians." [19] With him in office, Georgians believed they finally had the federal support they needed for a campaign to get rid of the Cherokee land claims once and for all.

Chapter 3

Cherokee Nation v. Georgia

URING THE 1820s, officials in Alabama, which had gained statehood in 1819, used threats and intimidation to pressure the Creek tribe into selling several million acres in the Chattahoochee River Valley to them. The episode reinforced the earlier lesson Georgians had learned from the incident with President Adams that aggressive action against the Indians produced results.

In 1828 the Georgia legislature declared that, by virtue of its original colonial charter, the state had the right to govern all land and people within its borders. This included the Cherokee. The federal treaties that guaranteed the Cherokee independence and ownership of territory had no bearing on Georgia, said the legislature, because the federal government had exceeded its authority in making them. Georgia claimed that the Constitution gave the federal government only the power to regulate commerce with the Cherokee.

"The Indians are tenants at Georgia's will," declared the lawmakers. "The lands in question belong to Georgia. She must and she will have them." [20]

Growing Pressure

At first, Georgia politicians issued this challenge simply as a warning. They were careful not to act too quickly or strongly against the Cherokee. After all, there were only fifteen thousand or so Cherokee up against nearly half a million whites in the largest state in the Union. Even Georgians who wanted the Cherokee removed reacted strongly against seeing such an underdog bullied or brutally oppressed. Georgia officials decided to wait and give President Jackson a chance to get the Cherokee to sell out peacefully.

Jackson had no better luck than his predecessors in producing a treaty in his first year. But he secretly offered Georgians some advice. "Build a fire under them," he wrote. "When it gets hot enough, they will move." [21] With that encouragement, Georgia embarked on a strategy of making the Cherokee so miserable they would have no choice but to depart. On June 30, 1830, the legislature outlawed the Cherokee government, nullified all its laws, and put the Cherokee under Georgia law. In December that same year the legislature created a special police force called the Georgia Guard to enforce its ban.

The Cherokee appealed to the federal government to step in on their behalf. After all, the United States had always recognized the Cherokee's land claims and right to govern themselves. This time, however, they found no sympathy. President Jackson said he could do nothing about the situation. Anything that took place within Georgia's borders, he said, was Georgia's business and the federal government could not interfere.

In July of 1829, gold was discovered along a creek in Cherokee territory. Rumors spread that Indian territory was filled with the precious metal. Many poor whites looked at gold as their only hope of becoming rich. By the middle of the following summer, more than three thousand white prospectors were trespassing on Cherokee land. Thousands more were clamoring for the government to take over Indian land so whites could have a chance at these riches.

At first, the federal government sent troops to protect the Cherokee from the trespassers. The soldiers were few and accomplished little. But even this token force offended Georgia. The state was determined to demonstrate that it was the final authority in all land within its borders. It asked Jackson to withdraw the troops. The president obliged. The troops were replaced by members of the Georgia Guard, who generally had no regard for Indians and looked the other way at abuses of their land and rights. The Georgia legislature made a difficult situation worse for the Cherokee by banning them from mining gold, even on their own land.

Indian Removal Act

Meanwhile, Jackson was working on another front to strengthen Georgia's hand. In his first address to the nation, he had urged the passage of the Indian Removal Act. This called for the federal government to coordinate the relocation of all Indians in lands west of the Mississippi River. Jackson did not propose to force the Indians out, but on the other hand, he warned that those who stayed would have to submit to the laws of the states in which their lands lay.

The nation was by no means united on the question of Indian policy. Many in the Northeast strongly opposed Jackson's removal act and were incensed by Georgia's actions against the Cherokee. Senator Theodore Frelinghuysen of New Jersey denounced the bill as a disgrace to the nation. "Is it one of the prerogatives of the white man," he asked, "that he may disregard the dictates of moral principles, when an Indian shall be concerned?" [22]

Senator Edward Everett.

Senator Edward Everett of Vermont pleaded with Georgia to back off its tough stance against the Cherokee. "If Georgia will recede," he said, "she will do more for the Union, and more for herself, than if she would add to her domain the lands of all the Indians, though they were paved in gold." [23]

Despite fierce opposition, the Indian Removal Act passed by a narrow margin in 1830. The Cherokee now found themselves cut off

SHARP KNIFE

Andrew Jackson was a man of action all his life. When he saw the potentially explosive stalemate between the Cherokee and Georgia settlers, he immediately set out to solve it.

Although they both advocated the same removal policy, Jackson's attitudes toward Indians were much different than Jefferson's. Jackson was a product of the western frontier, where clashes between settlers and Indians over many decades had created hard feelings. He claimed to love Native Americans, and even adopted a young Creek child whose parents had been killed by his troops in the Creek War. But he had little respect for them. Even as president, he constantly referred to them in a patronizing way, calling them "children of the forest."

Jackson set up a legal practice in Nashville, Tennessee, in 1788. In 1796, he went into politics and won election to the U.S. House of Representatives. He was appointed to the Senate the following year, but he suddenly dropped out in 1798. He claimed he could not afford to stay on the job, and instead got himself appointed as a judge in Tennessee.

Known as "Sharp Knife" to the Indians, Jackson was a fiery personality who functioned best in the heat of battle. He won his fame as major general of the Tennessee militia, a post he held from 1802 through 1815. By defeating both the Creek in Alabama, and the British in New Orleans shortly after in the final battle of the war in 1812, Jackson became the United States' most famous war hero of the age.

In 1815, he was appointed a federal Indian commissioner in the South. Over the next six years, according to one historian, "He and his fellow commissioners persuaded the tribes, by fair means or foul, to sell to the United States a major portion of their lands in the Southeast, including 1/5th of Georgia, 1/2 of Mississippi, and most of the area of Alabama. That Jackson and his relatives profited immensely from those sales is a matter of record."

Jackson ran for president as the champion of the common man in 1824. After falling just short in that election, he won the presidency in 1828. The Indian removal policy was the first item on his agenda, and he used all his power as president to get it passed in 1830. Even after the horrors that he set in motion with the forced removal of the Indians, Jackson continued to believe his plan had saved them. "It was a measure I had much at heart and sought to effect," he wrote, "because I was satisfied that the Indians could not possibly live under the laws of the states. . . . I feel confident of having done my duty to my red children."

from their main ally and protector; from here on, they could count on neither the president nor Congress to honor the promises of past treaties.

Cherokee Persecution

As months went by, Georgians built a larger and larger fire under the Cherokee. Hoping to pressure Cherokee leaders, many of whom were wealthy business owners and planters, into giving in, lawmakers passed legislation confiscating much of their property. They limited Cherokee land ownership to the lots on which their homes were built.

Most legal experts in the United States argued that these and other actions of the legislature against the Cherokee were illegal. But a state judge, A. S. Clayton, assured his fellow Georgians that they need not worry about the courts meddling in the Cherokee matter. "I only require the aid of public opinion and the arm of executive authority and no court on earth besides our own shall ever be troubled with this question," [24] he said.

On one occasion a state judge did rule in favor of the Cherokee. Georgia voters then tried to impeach the judge, and when that failed the legislature took away the courts' power to rule on matters involving Native Americans.

Despite the growing abuses and indignities, the Cherokee refused to give up their lands. The state of Georgia grew bolder in its contempt for Cherokee land claims. It divided Cherokee territory among several Georgia counties. It set up a lottery system to distribute Cherokee land to whites. Lottery winners began moving onto their new property even though the Cherokee had not agreed to sell.

Such contempt for Cherokee rights inevitably bred violence. A group of whites set a Cherokee farmer's horses loose after he refused to sell them. While the farmer ran to retrieve the horses, the whites broke into his house and beat his wife senseless. Georgians pushed Cherokee people off their farms and out of their homes and threatened or assaulted those who resisted. John Ross, one of the most influential of the Cherokee leaders, returned home from a trip to Washington, D.C., to find his family

A *chief refuses to allow passage through his land. Many Cherokee fought back when whites tried to take over their territories.*

forced out of their home and his farm and property taken by whites. None of these cases could ever go to court since, under Georgia law, the testimony of Indians against whites was not allowed.

The Georgia Guard, which was supposed to maintain law and order in Cherokee territory, were some of the worst offenders against Cherokee's rights. They tried to provoke Cherokee people into fighting back so they could arrest them. They charged on horseback at groups of Cherokee, sending them scattering for their lives. Some guardsmen mocked the religious ceremonies of Cherokee who had accepted Christianity. They interrupted one baptism ceremony by performing their own baptism on one of their horses.

People throughout the nation, including some Georgians, expressed outrage at the cruel treatment of the Cherokee. Andrew Jackson, however, refused to get involved. He insisted that

Even though Davy Crocket had courageously fought against Indians, he sided with those who opposed the Indian Removal Act.

Georgia had the right to govern all territory within its borders in any way that it chose.

Throughout all the persecution, the Cherokee held their ground. They refused to be goaded into violence, and they refused to sell their land. In the *Phoenix*, Elias Boudinot wrote, "Full license to our oppressors, and every avenue of justice closed to us. Yes, this is the bitter cup prepared for us by a republican and religious government—we shall drink it to the very dregs." [25] The Cherokee Nation clung to the hope that someone with authority in the United States would step forward and honor the treaties of the past.

INDIAN SUPPORTERS

The Cherokee had many supporters in Congress in their bid to retain their rights to self-government on their traditional lands. Three times, amendments intended to weaken the Indian Removal Act were defeated by a single vote.

The most respected of these supporters was Senator Theodore Frelinghuysen of New Jersey. A deeply religious man and distinguished lawyer who served as president of the American Board for Foreign Missions, the American Bible Society, and many other charitable groups, Frelinghuysen led the senate resistance to Jackson's Indian Removal Act. His passionate speech in defense of the Cherokee took him three days to deliver. When he was finished, even opponents admired his conviction and eloquence. His fight against Indian removal earned Frelinghuysen a national reputation that eventually landed him the vice presidential spot on a Whig ticket led by Henry Clay in 1844.

Most of the congressional votes against Jackson's policy came from the northeastern states. A glaring exception was a folksy backwoods congressman from the Tennessee frontier, Davy Crockett. Crockett started out as a farmer and Indian fighter in eastern Tennessee. After serving under Andrew Jackson in the Creek War, he moved to the western side of the state and got involved in politics. Ironically, Crockett was a staunch supporter of the rights of settlers and white land owners when he first won a seat in the Tennessee legislature in 1821.

His combination of fearless courage, honesty, and backwoods sense of humor earned him many admirers among the voters back home and in the nation's capital. He squandered a great deal of that good will, however, when he opposed his old commanding officer's Indian Removal Act. In his remarks on the subject, he admitted that most voters in his district disagreed with him and he apologized for being stubborn about the situation. But he believed that treaties signed with Indians were promises. If a person or a government could not live up to their promises, what good were they?

Crockett's brave stand cost him the support of many voters back home. In 1831, a year after the removal vote, Crockett was defeated for reelection. He gained back his seat in 1833 but lost again in 1835. Crockett became a national hero when he led a group of volunteers from Tennessee to help Texas fight for its freedom from Mexico in 1836 and was killed in the siege of the Alamo.

Last Resort

One of the Cherokee's most ardent defenders was the Reverend Jeremiah Evarts, a leading official of the American Board of Commissioners for Foreign Missions. His conscience stricken by the U.S. treatment of the Cherokee, Evarts believed that God would send a terrible calamity on the country if it did not right its wrongs.

Since Jackson was clearly opposed to the Cherokee and Congress had now gone on record against them in its Indian Removal vote, Evarts saw the Supreme Court as the nation's last hope to redeem its honor in Indian matters. Evarts had every confidence the Cherokee would prevail. "It is so clear a case that the court cannot mistake it," he told the Cherokee. "All the great lawyers in the country are on your side." [26]

He suggested a strategy for getting the Indians' concerns before the Supreme Court. He proposed that the Cherokee dig for gold on their territory. As this was against the new Georgia laws, they were certain to be arrested. The Cherokee could then sue for false imprisonment. Although the state court was certain to decide against them, they could then appeal the decision to the U.S. Supreme Court.

Although they declined his strategy, the Cherokee did seek legal advice, and the man they turned to was William Wirt. As a former U.S. attorney general in both the Monroe and John Quincy Adams administrations, Wirt was one of the most respected lawyers in the country. He was no stranger to controversy, having been one of the lawyers who defended former vice president Aaron Burr in his famous treason trial. He also believed strongly in the Cherokee's cause, and had publicly denounced the Indian Removal Act.

Wirt's first legal move was to file an appeal to the Supreme Court against Georgia's conviction of George Tassels. When Georgia short-circuited the case by moving up Tassels's execution, he fell back on a more general suit. Wirt asked the Supreme Court to issue a permanent injunction that would restrain Georgia from imposing its laws on the Cherokee Nation.

The illustrious William Wirt shocked President Jackson when he filed for an appeal to the Supreme Court.

Wirt's suit surprised and angered President Jackson. He denounced Wirt as a wicked man whose goal was to fleece the Cherokee Nation with huge legal fees. Instead of saving the Cherokee, predicted Jackson, Wirt would only accelerate their ruin.

Marshall's Dilemma

For more than thirty years, John Marshall had towered above his associates on the Supreme Court. He had built the Court up from a confused, weak cousin of the legislative and executive branches of the government to an emerging national presence.

Marshall had cultivated the Court's power with his intelligence, creativity, shrewdness, and fairness. However, there were occasions when the latter two traits ran into conflict, and the Cherokee suit was one of those. Marshall held a great deal of sympathy for the Indians' plight. He had nothing but disdain for the way the colonial and early U.S. governments had treated them and he believed that "oppression of a helpless people dependent on our magnanimity and justice for the preservation of their existence, impresses a deep stain on the American character." [27]

On the other hand, Marshall recognized that the Supreme Court's authority depended on two things. First, it must be seen as totally impartial. To ensure an unbiased reputation, Marshall steadfastly maintained that the Court's role was to enforce the Constitution, not make policy. That meant it had a duty to uphold any law not prohibited by the Constitution, even if it was a bad or unjust law. Second, the Court depended on Congress and the executive branch to accept and uphold its authority. Marshall recognized that either group might be tempted to disregard the Supreme Court if its decisions blatantly offended or outraged them. He worded opinions tactfully to avoid inflaming passions and tried to keep the Supreme Court out of partisan political fights.

The Cherokee case presented Marshall with a stew of confusing circumstances. He was well aware that the issues involved had generated one of the most heated and emotional debates in the history of Congress. He knew that President Jackson, who already held the Court in disdain because of previous opinions, bitterly opposed the suit, yet Marshall was convinced the Cherokee had been treated shamefully. He would have to tread carefully to make sure the justices reached a fair decision without provoking a political dogfight that could damage the Court's reputation.

Wirt Pleads His Case

Wirt's first task as the Cherokee's lawyer was to get the Supreme Court to agree to hear the case. Normally, the Court hears cases on appeal after they have first been tried in state or lower federal courts. Wirt did not want to get bogged down for years in lower courts while the Cherokee continued to suffer injustice. He

A faltering Supreme Court blossomed when John Marshall took control.

cited Article III, Section 2 of the Constitution, which gives the Supreme Court original jurisdiction (meaning the case can begin there) in cases to which a state is a party. Since the suit was filed against the state of Georgia, that requirement was met. The Supreme Court agreed to hear arguments on *Cherokee Nation v. Georgia* on March 5, 1831.

When the session began, however, only one party was present. Georgia had declined to send a representative. The state continued to insist that their dealings with the Cherokee inside their borders did not concern the federal government, and therefore the Supreme Court had no authority to hear the case. Georgia Senator Wilson Lumpkin put the matter bluntly when he said, "Georgia is not accountable to the Supreme Court or any other tribunal on earth." [28]

That left Wirt alone before the court. The veteran lawyer's task now became more difficult. The very section that he had cited in getting the Court to accept the case also limited the Court's role to disputes "between a State, or the Citizens thereof, and foreign States, Citizens, or Subjects." [29] Indians were not considered citizens of the United States. Therefore, the only grounds the Cherokee had for bringing a suit to the Court was as a foreign nation. The legal relationship between Native Americans and the United States had never been defined. Were the Cherokee a foreign nation? Wirt had to convince the Court that they were.

Appealing to plain logic, Wirt cited the United States' long history of signing treaties with Indians. The very nature of treaties was that they were agreements between two political bodies, or nations. It made no sense for a nation to sign a treaty except with another nation. By signing treaties with them, the United States had acknowledged that the Indian tribes were separate nations with legitimate governments with whom the United States could make agreements.

Wirt then went on to detail what these treaties promised. He cited the Treaty of Holston, signed by the United States on July 2, 1791, which said, "The United States solemnly guarantees to the Cherokee Nation all their lands not hereby ceded." [30]

That land, reminded Wirt, included the territory in northwest Georgia in which the Cherokee were being persecuted. "The boundaries were fixed by treaty, and what was within them was acknowledged to be the land of the Cherokees," he argued. "This was the scope of all the treaties." [31]

According to historian Samuel Carter III, "The more emotional an issue, the better [Wirt] could handle it," [32] and the in-

JOHNSON V. MCINTOSH: A HINT OF WHAT TO EXPECT

Prior to *Cherokee v. Georgia,* there had been only one Supreme Court case that had dealt in any way with issues of Indian territorial rights. The *Johnson v. McIntosh* case, which came before the Court in 1823, dealt with the legality of a grant of land that certain Indians had made to private individuals in 1773 and 1775. Federal laws enacted since that time banned any such private transactions of Indian land. The Court had to decide whether the Indians had possessed the right of ownership to the lands they had given away.

In deciding the case, Chief Justice John Marshall gave forewarning of what the Supreme Court's stance would be in the Cherokee cases. It was there that he first determined that Europeans' discovery of new lands gave them not unlimited ownership of all they claimed but only "the sole right of acquiring the soil from the natives." In his opinion, Marshall went on record as stating that Indian tribes had a legally protected right to their lands and that this right could be taken away only "by purchase or conquest." The decision, however, did not touch on whether the Court considered the Indians to have been conquered.

justices he saw inflicted on the Cherokee moved him passionately. Georgia was in clear violation of Cherokee rights of self-government and territory, he declared. "The legislation of Georgia proposes to annihilate [the Cherokee], as its very end and aim. . . . If those laws be fully executed, there will be no Cherokee nation, no Cherokee lands, no Cherokee treaties. . . . They will be swept out of existence together, leaving nothing but the monuments in our history of the enormous injustice that has been practised towards a friendly nation." [33]

The Court's Decision

The Cherokee waited anxiously for the Supreme Court ruling that they hoped would save their lands. On March 18, 1831, old John Marshall read the Court's decision in a barely audible voice. He began by admitting that the Cherokee had a valid complaint. "If courts were permitted to indulge their sympathies, a case better calculated to excite them can scarcely be imagined." [34]

He then dealt with Georgia's claim that Cherokee land belonged to Georgia by decree of the king of England. Marshall said that England's claim to the land had given that nation the right to acquire the land from the Cherokee, but did not give England clear title to the land.

Furthermore, he upheld the validity of U.S. treaties with the Indians, saying, "The words 'treaty' and 'nation' are words of our own language . . . having a definite and well-understood meaning. . . . We have applied them to Indians as we have applied them to the other nations of the earth." [35] Those treaties clearly gave the Cherokee the right to live on their land, free from Georgia's oppressive laws.

So far, so good for the Cherokee. But then Marshall took note of the peculiar fact that the Cherokee's territory lay within the boundaries of certain states and that the Cherokee had, according to treaties, put themselves under the protection of the United States. Neither of those situations described the normal circumstance of an independent nation.

The Cherokee, Marshall decided, were a "distinct political society, separated from others, capable of managing its own affairs and governing itself." [36] But were they a foreign nation? In a crushing defeat to the Cherokee, Marshall said they were not. Rather, he defined Native American tribes as "domestic dependent nations" whose "relationship to the United States resembles that of a ward to his guardian." [37] Because the Cherokee were a domestic dependent nation and not a foreign nation, they could not, under the Constitution, bring a suit before the Supreme Court.

"If it be true that wrongs have been inflicted and that still greater are to be apprehended," concluded Marshall, "this is not the tribunal which can redress the past or prevent the future." [38] By a four to two decision, the Court threw out the suit.

Marshall's Balancing Act

It appeared to be a typically masterful balancing act by Marshall. He did not want to put the Supreme Court in the position of dictating policy to the legislature of Georgia. That would get the Court too mixed up in politics, and there was every indication that Georgia would ignore the ruling anyway. Issuing rulings that no one heeded would only undermine the Court's authority.

On the other hand, he could not let the Court condone the treaty violations made by the state of Georgia. His opinion indicated that the Court considered the federal treaties legally binding on Georgia and that the state had overstepped its bounds in making the Cherokee subject to state law. Marshall's ruling to dismiss was not only legally correct, it allowed him to assert his moral principles and at the same time avoid any political consequences of that ruling by tossing out the case.

Chapter 4

Worcester v. Georgia

AFTER THEIR INITIAL disappointment, the Cherokee and their legal counsel detected a ray of hope in the Supreme Court's decision. Two of the justices, Smith Thompson and Joseph Story, had supported their case. Justice Thompson wrote a powerful and persuasive dissent that most experts consider his finest work in his years on the Court.

According to Thompson, the Supreme Court was obligated to decide the case because "The Constitution expressly gives the court jurisdiction in all cases of law and equity arising under the treaties made with the United States."[39] While admitting that "relief to the full extent prayed by the bill may be beyond the reach of this court,"[40] Thompson insisted that the Cherokee's complaint was valid. He argued that the Cherokee were, in fact, a foreign nation. "They have always been dealt with as such by the government of the United States, both before and since the adoption of the present Constitution,"[41] he noted. The many wars between Native Americans and whites had not changed the status of the Indians, Thompson observed, because the wars had all ended, not in conquest, but with treaties.

That being the case, Thompson made it clear that he was on the side of the Cherokee Nation. Despite the quibbling about the legal status of the Indians, Thompson said that the treaties signed by the United States left no question that "there is as full and complete recognition of their sovereignty, as if they were absolute owners of the soil. That they are entitled to such occupancy, so long as they choose quietly and peaceably to remain on the land, cannot be questioned."[42] Thompson left no doubt that he considered Georgia's laws to be violations of Cherokee rights that the United States had solemnly sworn to uphold.

Hints of Better Luck Next Time

Since Thompson's arguments were on the losing side of the Supreme Court vote, they normally would not have carried much weight. But he was joined in his dissent by Joseph Story, who was not only the most respected associate justice on the Court but was also a close friend of John Marshall. For Story and the chief justice to be on opposing sides in a vote was almost unheard of.

Thompson's and Story's passionate appeals on behalf of the Cherokee touched a nerve with Marshall and made him uncomfortable with the legal technicality that he had used to avoid ruling in the case. It was he, in fact, who persuaded Thompson to publish his dissent, which the justice had previously kept to himself. For as much as he wanted to avoid the political nightmare that a decision in the Cherokee case would surely bring, Marshall was a courageous man of unshakable moral character. As historian Anthony F. C. Hobson writes, "His efforts to separate law from politics never entailed sacrificing legal rights in order to avoid political conflict."[43]

Marshall had made clear even in throwing out the Cherokee case that he thought justice was on the side of the Indians regarding their treaty rights. Goaded by Story, Thompson, and his own conscience, Marshall privately expressed second thoughts about

Joseph Story (top), Smith Thompson (bottom).

having taken what he admitted was "a very narrow view"[44] of the law. In his opinion in *Cherokee Nation v. Georgia*, he had given strong hints that if some way could be found to get a suit before the Supreme Court that could meet all the standards required by the Constitution, there was a reasonable chance the Cherokee would win a favorable ruling. He was itching for a chance to take a stand that would put the Supreme Court squarely on the side of justice in this matter.

The Missionary Law

Since Marshall had ruled out Native Americans as a party to a suit against Georgia, the Cherokee needed to find an American citizen to press charges. But in order for the suit to have legal standing before the Supreme Court, that citizen could not sue on behalf of the Cherokee. He or she had to petition on their own behalf. But how could a white person claim to be hurt by Georgia's laws against the Cherokee?

The Cherokee and their legal counsel found the answer to that in one of the many laws that Georgia passed in the attempt to extend their control over Cherokee land. In December of 1830, the state passed a law making it illegal for white persons to live in Cherokee territory without a license from the governor. The penalty for violating this law was a four-year prison term at hard labor. Although some lawmakers claimed that the law's purpose was to protect the Cherokee from the swarm of gold miners trespassing on their land, the law was really aimed at northern missionaries.

Georgia politicians were stung by harsh criticism from the Northeast over their policies. The criticism made them suspicious of missionaries sent by religious groups in that part of the country to work among the Indians of the South. Political leaders such as Wilson Lumpkin became convinced that these missionaries were encouraging the Cherokee to resist giving up their lands.

Jailing the Missionaries

The Cherokee's legal counsel saw that the law gave them the opportunity they were looking for. Here was a law aimed at U.S.

THE OTHER JUSTICES IN *WORCESTER*

The only other justice on the Supreme Court during the Cherokee cases who gained widespread respect for his work was Joseph Story. Born in 1779, Story grew up in the fishing village of Marblehead, Massachussetts. He gained fame as a legal genius and quickly became one of the rising stars in Jefferson's Democratic-Republican party that gradually took over control of the government from the Federalists. His future as a legislator with that party ended, however, when Story voted with the Federalists on legislation that Jefferson desperately wanted.

Story won a spot on the Supreme Court in 1810 only because President James Madison could not find anyone else to take the job. After his first three choices for the Court all declined, Madison reluctantly nominated Story. When Jefferson, a close friend of Madison's, heard of the choice, he flew into a rage.

At thirty-two, Story was the youngest person ever appointed to the Supreme Court. Story and Marshall became such close friends that many described their relationship as that of a father and son. Story's remarkable insight proved invaluable in helping Marshall steer the Court through turbulent times. It was Story who wrote the controversial decision in *Martin v. Hunter's Lessee* in which the Supreme Court claimed the authority to review state judicial decisions.

Smith Thompson had been on the Court for eight years at the time of his *Cherokee v. Georgia* dissent. He was an able politician in his own right, and he created something of a stir by running for governor of New York while still serving on the Supreme Court.

William Johnson was a Jefferson appointee who served thirty years on the Supreme Court without distinguishing himself. Gabriel Duval was appointed to the Court in 1811 by Madison. The fact that neither was able to stand up to Marshall and Story was a source of irritation to both Jefferson and Madison. At the time of the Cherokee cases, they were both at the end of long and relatively unnoteworthy stints on the Court.

The final two members of the Court, John McLean and Henry Baldwin, were both recent appointees of Andrew Jackson. McLean showed remarkable independence in breaking with Jackson on the issue of Indian treaty rights. Baldwin sided with Jackson, the only justice to do so. Known as an abrasive personality, Baldwin frequently clashed with his colleagues on the Court. His dissent in the *Worcester* case was not unusual. During 1831, he violated Marshall's long-standing desire for Court solidarity by dissenting from the majority on seven different cases.

On December 13, 1830, a law was passed which prohibited white people from living on Cherokee land without a license. This law affected missionaries because they were no longer able to live among the Cherokee.

citizens living in Indian territory. Here was a case that Marshall could not throw out! Any citizen prosecuted under the law had a right to challenge its constitutionality before the Supreme Court. If only they could find someone willing to risk going to prison for the sake of the cause.

While some missionaries left Cherokee land rather than expose themselves to such a law, many did not. In July of 1831, the Georgia Guard arrested eleven missionaries living in Cherokee territory. Among them was Samuel Worcester. Originally from Vermont, Worcester had been superintendent of an Indian school, one of the founders of the *Cherokee Phoenix*, and a staunch opponent of Indian removal.

The arrest of the missionaries and their harsh treatment while being marched away in chains by the Georgia Guard left Georgia with a knotty problem. Already its citizens were sensitive to the state's image as a ruthless oppressor of Indians. Throwing missionaries, of all people, in jail was exactly the kind of public relations nightmare the state did not need. Many prominent Georgia citizens spoke up on behalf of the missionaries.

When Worcester asked to be released, Judge Augustin Clayton was able to find a loophole that allowed him to oblige.He noted that Worcester was an employee of the federal government and declared that he therefore was not subject to state law regarding Indian lands.

Hard-line politicians such as Governor Gilmer, however, had no sympathy whatsoever for the missionaries. Gilmer contacted the federal government and demanded to know if Worcester was indeed a federal employee. The answer came back that, technically, he was, because he had been commissioned as postmaster at the Cherokee capital of New Echota. But, at the governor's request,

A phoenix is shown here rising from flames. Samuel Worcester, one of the missionaries arrested on July of 1831, was also one of the founders of the Cherokee Phoenix.

President Jackson solved that problem simply by firing him from his post.

Worcester Takes a Stand

All eleven missionaries were convicted by the Georgia courts in September 1831. But, still anxious to avoid the scathing criticism pouring in from around the nation, the governor offered to give the missionaries a pardon and their freedom if they would either swear an oath to Georgia, which meant they would respect even its harsh laws against the Cherokee, or leave the territory. Only Worcester and a medical missionary, Dr. Elizur Butler, declined either option. They held fast to their conviction that they were subject only to Cherokee laws while on Cherokee land.

Worcester wrote that his conscience had given him no other choice. "[I] f I suffer in consequence of continuing to preach the gospel and diffuse the written word of God among this people, I trust that I shall be sustained by a conscience void of offense, and by the anticipation of a righteous decision at that tribunal from which there is no appeal." [45]

While Worcester and Butler were delivered to prison to begin serving hard labor, the Cherokee's lawyer, William Wirt, and his associate, John Sargent, filed a suit with the Supreme Court against the state of Georgia. In November of 1831, the Court issued a citation asking representatives of the state of Georgia to appear before it and show why the judgment against Worcester should not be overruled. The governor of Georgia submitted copies of the Court's citation to the state legislature, which ordered him to disregard it. The Supreme Court agreed to hear the *Worcester v. Georgia* case on February 20, 1832, with the decision to apply to Butler's situation as well.

The Arguments

As in the *Cherokee v. Georgia* case, the state of Georgia refused to present arguments to the court. Still convinced that federal courts had no business interfering with state laws, Georgia officials made it clear that they intended to ignore any decision the Court might reach.

While the case specifically concerned Georgia's violation of Samuel Worcester's rights in forcing him to obtain a license in order to live in Cherokee country, William Wirt made certain to

THE MISSIONARY INFLUENCE

The *Worcester* case would never have been possible without the involvement of a group of people who were primarily motivated by religion, not politics. During the first half of the nineteenth century, many Americans felt the call of conscience to work for the betterment of society. Dozens of reform societies sprang up in the North and East dedicated to such issues as peace, antislavery, women's rights, and the banning of alcohol. One of these societies was the American Board of Commissioners for Foreign Missions.

The American Board was the brainchild of a group of students at the Andover Theological Seminary in Massachussetts. In 1810, they formed the organization, modeled after the British and Foreign Bible Society, for the purpose of spreading the Christian message among unchurched people throughout the world. The British mission societies had been especially noteworthy for their work among Native Americans. They had provided valuable support for Indians seeking to uphold their treaty rights.

The timing of the Board's creation was fortunate. Following the British defeat in the War of 1812, British missionary societies pulled out of the Indian territory. Without their support, Indians found themselves fighting an often lonely battle against the encroachments of settlers. The Congregational and Presbyterian ministers sent into Indian areas by the American Board filled the void.

The American Board believed that, while they fed the Indians' souls by translating the Bible and preaching the Gospel, they also needed to improve their everyday lives by building schools and hospitals. Supporting the Cherokee in their quest for justice was just another expression of this philosophy.

American Board missionaries such as Samuel Worcester persuaded many Cherokee to adopt the Christian faith. Cherokee people built churches in their villages and sent a number of their young men, including *Cherokee Phoenix* publisher Elias Boudinot, to seminaries.

Following the removal of the Cherokee, the American Board's efforts went largely overseas. By 1877, it directed the efforts of 375 missionaries. The work of the American Board continues today as part of the United Church Board for World Missions, into which the Board merged in 1961.

call into question the legality of all the Georgia laws regarding Cherokee land. He polished some of the arguments he had presented in the previous Supreme Court case as to why Georgia's laws were violations of federal treaties. In all of the treaties, he explained, the United States had recognized the Cherokee Nation as a sovereign nation, with the right and ability to govern itself. Nothing had changed since the signing of those treaties, said Wirt, to alter that circumstance. Therefore, the United States should step in and enforce the treaties against Georgia's attempt to take over the governing of the Cherokee.

Cannot Give Away What They Do Not Own

As in the *Cherokee* case, John Marshall wrote and announced the decision of the Court. This time, however, on March 3, 1832, he delivered a lengthy, strongly worded, tightly reasoned argument that ruled in favor of Worcester. In the Court's view, not only was the Georgia law which targeted missionaries a violation of federal treaties, so were all of Georgia's laws which claimed authority over Cherokee territory.

Marshall began by covering some of the same ground he had gone over in the earlier case. He noted that to support its claim of control over Cherokee lands, Georgia cited its charter and the Treaty of Paris, signed in 1783 at the end of the Revolution, that transferred all of Great Britain's territorial claims in eastern North America to the United States. Marshall expressed disdain for the claim that "discovery" gave European nations rights to North America that "annulled the pre-existing rights of its ancient possessors."[46] He rejected the idea that people could suddenly claim to be the owners of land halfway around the world just because they had not previously known of its existence.

Georgia's original charter, then, was "granted by the monarch of a distant and distinct region, parceling out territory in possession of others whom he could not and did not attempt to move."[47] It was only valid against the claims of other Europeans, not against the claims of Indians. As for the treaty of 1783 with Great Britain, Marshall pointed out, Great Britain could not give away rights that it did not have.

Full Right to Lands They Occupy

Marshall emphasized again that Indian tribes "had always been considered as distinct, independent political communities, retaining their original natural rights, as the undisputed possessors of the soil."[48] The Indians had never surrendered those rights through conquest because they had never been conquered. All conflicts had been resolved by treaties which laid out the relationship that existed between all parties concerned.

After reviewing the history of those treaties and trade agreements between the United States and Indians, Marshall concluded that all of them "manifestly consider the Indian nations as distinct political communities, having territorial boundaries, within which their authority is exclusive."[49] Marshall argued that Georgia had never taken issue with the terms "nation" and "treaty" in reference to dealing with Indians. This proved, said Marshall, that Georgia went along with the clearly expressed conviction that the Cherokee's claim to their lands were valid.

Marshall then had to deal with the issue he had brought up in his earlier definition of Indian tribes not as foreign nations but as domestic dependent nations. As he had outlined in his earlier opinion, the Indians had, in the course of treaty negotiations, surrendered some of their land claims and some of their rights. For example, the treaties prohibited trade or treaties with nations other than the United States. Later treaties also put the Indians to some degree under the protection of the U.S. government. Under such conditions, were the Indians still to be considered independent nations with governments that could legitimately own territory and sign treaties?

Of course, said Marshall. In his view, it was a well-established legal principle that just because a group chooses to associate with a stronger one does not mean it surrenders its independence. As undisputed possessors of the soil, the tribes were within their rights to negotiate away certain of their rights and to keep others. The fact that they traded away some rights did not diminish the value of the rights they kept.

In answer to those who said the federal government had no right to interfere with the affairs of Georgia, Marshall said that it

JOHN MARSHALL:
AGING GIANT OF THE SUPREME COURT

John Marshall, according to historians Robert Carp and Ronald Stidham, "brought a first-class mind and a thoroughly engaging personality into second-class company." He so dominated the Supreme Court in its early years that he was able to shape it into his image of a powerful instrument of justice at a time when most political leaders were suspicious of giving power to the federal government.

Born in Germantown, Virginia, in 1755, Marshall studied law and set up a legal practice in Virginia. He enlisted in the army of his father's old friend, George Washington, during the American Revolution. His belief in a strong federal government was forged in the ice and misery of Valley Forge during the winter of 1777–78. He thought that his fellow soldiers would not have had to endure starvation and freezing had a central government been in charge of the operations instead of a collaboration of sometimes quarreling colonies. "I went into the Revolution a Virginian," he once said, "and came out an American."

Marshall enjoyed a distinguished political career after the war. He won three terms in the Virginia legislature, served as special diplomat to France, and was elected to the U.S. Congress. In 1800, President John Adams appointed him secretary of state. The following year, Adams added him to the Supreme Court, making him the only person ever to serve two such important government positions at the same time.

By the force of his personality and intelligence, he steadily built respect and authority for the Supreme Court. It was Marshall who persuaded the justices to abandon the tradition of each giving his own opinion. Instead, one justice delivered the "opinion of the Court," and dissenting opinions were discouraged unless it was absolutely a matter of principle. More often than not, it was Marshall himself who wrote the opinion of the Court, amazing both friends and enemies with his ability to find a clear and simple answer for the most complex cases.

Marshall's belief in a strong federal government infuriated presidents such as Thomas Jefferson and Andrew Jackson, who favored states' rights. Jackson and Marshall were particularly bitter enemies. Marshall, who normally stayed out of politics, personally campaigned against Jackson in presidential elections. By the time of the Cherokee cases, Marshall was seventy-six years old and in poor health. Yet he stayed on the Court, hoping to outlive Jackson's presidency and thus deny the president the chance to replace him on the Court.

Marshall failed in that goal, dying of liver disease in 1835 with Jackson still in office. But his effect on the Supreme Court and the nation was so great that former president Adams once declared, "My gift of John Marshall to the people of the United States was the proudest act of my life."

was Georgia that was interfering with the affairs of the nation. Georgia's laws, he said, "interfere forcibly with the relationship established between the United States and the Cherokee nation, the regulation of which, according to the settled principles of our constitution, are committed exclusively to the government of the union."[50]

Setting aside his usual tact, Marshall called the Georgia laws "repugnant to the Constitution."[50] Answering Georgia's claim that the Supreme Court had no right to interfere with matters inside Georgia's boundaries, Marshall said that the Court was bound to act. Georgia's laws had to be overturned because they interfered with U.S.-Cherokee relations, in clear violation of the Constitution's delegation of powers.

Marshall summed up the case by saying, "The Cherokee Nation, then, is a distinct community, occupying its own territory, within boundaries accurately described, in which the laws of Georgia can have no force."[52] The Court stood nearly unanimous in its decision in favor of Worcester and the Cherokee Nation. Marshall, Story, and Thompson were joined by William Johnson, Gabriel Duval, and John McLean. Only Henry Baldwin, whom President Jackson had appointed to the court, disagreed with the opinion.

Henry Baldwin.

Within two days of the decision, Marshall issued a formal order to the Georgia Supreme Court to reverse its decision and set Worcester and Butler free.

Georgia: No Response

After years of frustration in dealing with the United States, the Cherokee were pleasantly astounded that they won the court case. Most of the tribe rejoiced at finally finding a U.S.

government authority that would honor the nation's treaty promises. An editorial in the *Phoenix* proclaimed, "The question is forever settled as to who is right and who is wrong. It is not now between the great state of Georgia and the poor Cherokee, but between the United States and the State of Georgia."[53] It was natural to expect that the larger and more powerful of the two governments would prevail.

Some of the more experienced Cherokee leaders, however, cautioned against celebrating. They knew better than to think the matter could be settled so quickly and easily. They had seen Georgia's determination to get Cherokee land and knew the state had powerful allies in the federal government, particularly President Jackson.

Georgia's response to the court order was no surprise to the Cherokee leaders. The state simply ignored the ruling. It managed to do so, however, in a way that did not openly provoke the federal government. The Georgia Supreme Court had adjourned until 1833. During the crucial first months following the decision, no judge was on duty to carry out the order to release Worcester or to rescind the Cherokee laws. Even when the Georgia court reconvened the following year, it never acknowledged in writing its refusal to obey the ruling. It simply did nothing. Worcester and Butler languished in jail. The Georgia state lottery to distribute Cherokee lands went on as scheduled. White settlers continued to take Cherokee lands and property without fear of punishment.

Enforcing the Supreme Court's Decision

While political observers expected Georgia would ignore the Court, the crucial issue was what the federal government would do. At that time, there was not yet a national consensus as to the authority of the Supreme Court. Were the states obligated to obey the directives of the Court in cases where they believed it was meddling in state affairs? Were Congress and the president required to enforce whatever opinions the seven old gentlemen on the Court issued? If so, how were they to go about it? How does one force a state to stop enforcing its own laws? Should the government take the drastic step of sending an army to storm the Georgia prison and release Worcester and Butler? Would it have to take over Georgia's government, risking civil war?

All eyes turned to President Jackson to see what he would do. The answer seemed clearcut. It was no secret that the president's sympathies lay with Georgia. He had repeatedly expressed his view that Georgia had an absolute right to rule as it saw fit within its borders. The president had encouraged Georgia's oppression of the Cherokee every step of the way. The Supreme Court's opinion that Georgia's laws had no force in Cherokee territory was a direct slap at Jackson's Indian relocation policy, which stated that all Indians who refused to move would be at the mercy of state laws.

Furthermore, Jackson had a long history of conflict with John Marshall over federal court rulings. When the Supreme Court ruled against him on some banking issues, the president made no secret of his displeasure. Knowing Jackson's feelings, many people assumed Jackson would defy the Supreme Court's decision in this case. Word leaked out that Jackson greeted news of the *Worcester* decision with a derisive, "Well, John Marshall has made his decision. Now let him enforce it." [54]

There is no proof that Jackson said any such thing, and recent historians have doubted that he did. Jackson had many enemies who wanted to cripple him politically. The Cherokee matter was one of the more explosive issues on which a large share of the population vigorously disagreed with the president. His enemies were not above seizing the issue and exaggerating Jackson's role as an oppressor of Indians. Jackson himself believed the court cases were politically motivated and part of a broad campaign against him.

In truth, Jackson found himself walking an unexpectedly dangerous tightrope.

Chapter 5

Results of the Cherokee Cases

PRESIDENT JACKSON HAD been so intent on carrying out his Indian removal policy that he had encouraged, supported, and even advised Georgia in its campaign to ignore federal treaties. In the wake of the *Worcester* case, however, it became apparent that Georgia had opened up a Pandora's box of potential disasters for the U.S. government, of which Jackson was the leader.

South Carolina's Nullification Movement

As Georgia defied the Supreme Court decision without any penalty, other states grew bold in asserting that their laws took priority over those of the federal government. Alabama and Mississippi extended their state laws over Indian lands within their borders. South Carolina then moved toward the next step, an idea called nullification.

South Carolina's complaint was with a federal tax called a tariff. The federal government imposed a tariff beginning in 1816 on manufactured goods coming into the country. By 1830, most imported goods were taxed at least a third and sometimes as much as half their value. The tariff's purpose was to help new factories in the United States compete against British-manufactured products. The problem was that most of the new American factories were in New England. Agricultural states such as South Carolina received little benefit from the tariff, while their citizens had to pay a large tax on imported goods. Citizens of South Carolina

72

grew so irate at paying this money that they began to champion the idea of nullification. The state's politicians claimed that states had the right to nullify or disregard federal laws they did not like.

In effect, this was exactly what Georgia was doing regarding the *Worcester* decision. However, even Georgians were concerned about the extremes to which South Carolina was going. Although Georgians wanted the Cherokee removed from their borders, they were not prepared to accept the chaos that would result if each state could pick and choose which federal laws to obey. Neither was Andrew Jackson.

Limited Options

Jackson now saw that if he let Georgia defy the Supreme Court ruling, he would give South Carolina ammunition to use in its nullification campaign. On the other hand, if he strongly enforced the Court's decision, he would derail his cherished Indian-removal policy.

Historians such as Ronald Satz argue that Jackson could not have much done about the situation even if he had wanted to. "Enforcement of the decision in *Worcester v. Georgia* was impossible under existing law,"[55] according to Satz. Congress made an attempt at the end of 1831 to give the Supreme Court some clout. The House of Representatives debated a resolution that would direct the federal government to take action to enforce decisions of the Supreme Court. The nation was widely split on this matter, along the same lines as the split over Indian policy. Many in the Northeast wanted strong federal enforcement, while those in the South and West opposed the idea. As with the Indian Removal Act, the South and West had just enough votes to prevail. The resolution was tabled by a vote of ninety-nine to eighty-nine.

That left Jackson with limited options. Without some action from Congress, Jackson would have been in opposition to the Constitution had he moved aggressively against Georgia. It was this lack of congressional authorization to enforce Court decisions that led Jackson to comment, "The decision of the Supreme Court has fell stillborn."[55]

The president, however, was not completely powerless. His influence among the leaders of Georgia was so great that one North Carolina congressman said, "General Jackson could by a nod of the head or a crook of the finger induce Georgia to submit to the law." [57]

Behind-the-Scenes Manuevering

Ordinarily a man of bold action, Jackson moved cautiously on the *Worcester* matter. He used his influence to get Georgia to follow the letter of the law in the *Worcester* case without disturbing his Indian removal plans. His administration, most notably Secretary of State Martin Van Buren, worked behind the scenes to arrange a compromise that would allow Georgia to release the missionaries without upsetting Jackson's relocation policy.

The intrepid Andrew Jackson had to be cautious in his handling of the Worcester *case.*

William Wirt had wanted to file an appeal that would force the federal government to take action to release Worcester and Butler. But the imprisoned missionaries came under a great deal of pressure from people who feared what would happen to the Union if the federal government moved against Georgia. When even the American Board of Commissioners for Foreign Missions failed to back the missionaries' further fight, the two men decided to give in. In December 1832, Worcester and Butler agreed to end their legal actions against the state of Georgia. In exchange, the governor of Georgia issued a pardon for them on January 10, 1833. Four days later, they were released.

This masterful stroke of negotiating allowed Jackson to escape his dilemma. He had taken action, however slight, in support of the Supreme Court's order that Worcester and Butler must be released. He pushed Georgia away from the position of openly opposing the federal government. This gave him firmer ground to stand on in maintaining a stable federal government and in opposing South Carolina's nullification movement.

At the same time, Jackson had allowed Georgia to save face by accomplishing the release through a governor's pardon. Georgia could claim that it had not yielded to the Supreme Court but had voluntarily agreed to show mercy to the missionaries. Most Georgians, uncomfortable with their state's conflict with the federal courts, approved of the pardon and breathed a sigh of relief at the release. Hardliners, however, blasted the governor as one who, "in the case of the missionaries, did, by his conduct, sacrifice the dignity of the State and prove himself incapable of sustaining her honor." [58]

The only losers in the situation were the Cherokee. While Jackson arranged the release of the missionaries, he did absolutely nothing to enforce the Court's verdict that Georgia's laws against the Cherokee were illegal.

Dead End

By 1833, a cloud of depression lingered over the Cherokee. They had appealed to the highest court in the land and won. They had gained the sympathy of John Marshall, the most powerful legal figure in the nation's history. Marshall had, as one analyst said, "stretched the limits of judicial power as far as he could in *Worcester* to give the Cherokee tribe's legal claims a full hearing at the Supreme Court." [59] Yet nothing had changed. With the Supreme Court unable to make Georgia comply with its ruling, and with the Congress and the president firmly in favor of removal, the Cherokee had nowhere to turn for the defense of their homeland.

Georgia stepped up its campaign of intimidation to evict the Cherokee from their lands. Cherokee people were routinely beaten, whipped, robbed, and had their lands confiscated by whites. The only question appeared to be how much suffering the Cherokee would take before they either gave in or were wiped out as a tribe. A frustrated William Wirt admitted nothing more could be done on the legal front. Indian allies in Congress and on the mission boards sadly advised them to make the best deal they could for relocating. Eager to bring this controversial chapter in his administration to a quick end, Jackson offered several million dollars to the Cherokee in addition to title to their new lands. Even Justice John McLean, who had joined Marshall in ruling in favor of the Cherokee in *Worcester,* advised the Cherokee to sign a removal treaty.

In their long struggle to hold on to their guaranteed treaty rights, the Cherokee had reached a dead end.

Minority Treaty

Their hopeless state of affairs caused a rift in the Cherokee Nation. While some became resigned to making the best of a bad situation, others declared they would sooner die than voluntarily give up their homeland. Their determination increased when they saw the fate of their former enemy, the Creek. Although the Creek had agreed to removal terms, the process proved to be extremely harsh and cruel. Their lands and property were taken from them well before the actual removal, leaving them without food crops. Their possessions were stolen along the way, and many people were struck down by disease. Creek warriors and even old men were put in chains, mounted on ponies, and crammed together on riverboats. One overloaded boat capsized, drowning hundreds of Creek tribe members.

MARSHALL'S INFLUENCE: 166 YEARS LATER

While John Marshall's opinion in *Worcester v. Georgia* failed to protect the Cherokee of Georgia, it continues to provide a legal shield for modern Native Americans. Recently, residents of Minnesota engaged in a heated debate over fishing rights at Lake Mille Lacs, one of the state's prime walleye-fishing spots. The Mille Lacs band of the Chippewa tribe claimed fishing rights free from state regulations based on an 1837 treaty with the United States. In 1990, they sued in federal court to challenge Minnesota's authority to regulate their hunting and fishing rights on 13 million acres of public land in central Minnesota. Seven other Chippewa bands in Minnesota and Wisconsin joined as parties to the suit. In a dramatic switch from the Jackson-era indifference and downright hostility, the federal government supported the Indians in their suit.

A federal judge and the Eighth U.S. Circuit Court of Appeals both sided with the Indians. In another ironic turnaround from the Cherokee cases, this time it was the state appealing to the Supreme Court in an attempt to gain a favorable ruling.

Minnesota's popular governor, Jesse Ventura, declared any Indians who tried to claim treaty rights "ought to be back in birch-bark canoes." The state's attorneys argued before the Supreme Court that the Chippewa hunting and fishing rights had been invalidated by two events. First, President Zachary Taylor had revoked them when he had ordered the Indians off the land in 1850. (In yet another irony, it was the Indians who this time ignored the federal order, which the government never enforced.) Second, the state's attorney argued that the rights had been canceled when Minnesota became a state in 1858.

On March 23, 1999, the Supreme Court announced a five to four decision in favor of the Indians. Writing for the majority, Sandra Day O'Connor said, "After an examination of the historical record, we conclude that the Chippewa retain the rights guaranteed to them under the 1837 treaty." She said that neither President Taylor nor the state had the power to take away those rights. Following the path pioneered by John Marshall long ago, she said that such rights could be revoked only when Congress clearly stated its intent to do so.

In August 1834, the Cherokee council, still meeting despite Georgia's ban, overwhelmingly removed several top Cherokee leaders from office for advocating a treaty that would accept removal. In late December of the following year, some of these rejected leaders helped organize a council in the Cherokee capital of New Echota for the purpose of signing a relocation treaty. Fewer than four hundred

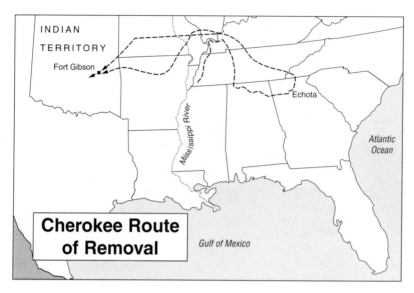

Cherokee Route of Removal

Cherokee attended the meeting. Nonetheless, those present signed a treaty in which they gave up their eastern lands in exchange for the U.S. government's offer of lands in the west and $5 million.

The Treaty of New Echota was forwarded to the U.S. Senate for ratification. Another stormy debate over Indian policy followed. The Cherokee's main leader, John Ross, argued that the treaty was invalid. Neither he nor other key Cherokee government officials had signed it, and the majority of the people opposed it. His arguments persuaded such influential statesmen as Daniel Webster, Henry Clay, and John Calhoun that the treaty was bogus. But with Andrew Jackson applying all the pressure of his position on wavering senators, the Senate ratified the Treaty of New Echota by a single vote. On May 23, 1836, Jackson signed it into law. He made it clear that this was one treaty that the federal government would enforce with all the power at its disposal. The Cherokee had two years to get out of Georgia peaceably. After that, the U.S. Army would move them.

The Trail of Tears

John Ross continued to fight against the treaty. At one point, Martin Van Buren, who replaced Jackson as president in 1836, offered to postpone the removal deadline two years. But he backed down when Georgia objected and raised an army of two thousand to enforce the treaty themselves.

When the removal deadline arrived, most of the Cherokee still clung to their lands in Georgia. The federal government sent General Winfield Scott at the head of seven thousand troops to round up the Cherokee and escort them on their way. It was an assignment that Scott detested in every way, and he ordered his men to treat the Cherokee with the utmost respect and kindness. The soldiers for the most part obeyed, but he could not control the scavengers who hovered near the camps, ready to run off with any possessions the Cherokee could not carry away.

After being detained in wretched camps, thirteen ragtag groups of Cherokee set off at different intervals on a march eight hundred miles to the west. One group stopped for a month in Missouri because they were too sick to continue. More than four thousand Cherokee died of starvation, exposure, and disease on a journey that came to be known as "The Trail of Tears."

The Cherokee, deprived of their territories, were forced into squalid camps. General Winfield Scott opposed such treatment and wanted the Indians to be treated with respect.

But by this time, the public had tired of the Cherokee's long battle. The horrendous conditions of the Trail of Tears march provoked no public outcry against removal. Georgia's political leaders boasted that the state was free to march into a new era of prosperity now that it had finally unsnarled the complex problem of Cherokee trespassers.

Indian Territory

When the Cherokee arrived in the Indian Territory of Oklahoma to join the sixty or so tribes already living there, they tried to regroup as a nation. But as historian Anthony F. C. Wallace said, the Cherokee removal "was a disaster that never really ended." [60] The Cherokee continued to run into deceit and fraud at the hands of whites, who took advantage of their poverty to gain control of their land.

In 1839, a bitter split between those who had urged relocation and those who had fought it led to the murders of three of the most active pro-relocation Cherokee, including *Phoenix* editor Elias Boudinot. The scars of this strife were still healing when the Cherokee were divided even further over what course to take in the Civil War. The majority of Cherokee men made the disastrous decision to fight on the side of the Confederacy, which further alienated the tribe from the federal government.

The federal government then changed its policy so that Indian Territory land was given not to the tribe, as befit Cherokee culture, but was parceled out among individuals. The desperately poor Cherokee landowners were preyed upon by unscrupulous whites. By the time Indian Territory was dissolved and reorganized as the state of Oklahoma in 1907, the Cherokee had lost virtually all of the lands granted to them in exchange for their eastern lands. In Wallace's words, "The Indian Territory became a vast, poverty-stricken concentration camp, administered by a federal bureaucracy—the Bureau of Indian Affairs, created by Jackson's presidential directives." [61]

Remarkably, the Cherokee Nation has held together and prospered despite the fact that it controlled no territory. Currently, the western tribe of Cherokee numbers roughly 165,000 people.

Most Indians decided to fight against the Union.

Meanwhile, slightly more than ten thousand Cherokee continue to live near their traditional lands in the Smoky Mountain foothills of western North Carolina. Some of these are the descendents of a group of Cherokee who had bought parcels of land in North Carolina and so were not subject to removal. Others are descendants of those who fled into the Smoky Mountains during the Trail of Tears roundup and were never caught.

Legacy of the Cherokee Cases

The tragic story of the Cherokee immediately following the *Worcester* and *Cherokee* decisions leaves the distinct impression that these were utterly meaningless court cases. But in fact, legal experts cite Marshall's decision in *Worcester* as "one of the five most frequently cited cases of the pre–Civil War era." [62]

While the Cherokee cases did not stop the removal of Indians to the west, they have had a profound effect on Indian relations in the United States. In *Cherokee Nation v. Georgia*, Marshall established the legal definition of the relationship between Native Americans and the United States. From that time forward, the United States would consider Indian tribes as separate nations, but also dependent domestic nations subject to the authority of the United States.

Marshall's opinion established the principle that the federal government's treaties with Indians were binding upon the entire nation. At a time when a sizable segment of the population, including President Jackson, believed the nation should simply take Indian land, the Court said that such actions were illegal under the Constitution.

Whether they agreed with Marshall or not, U.S. politicians accepted the Court's position. Historian Charles Wilkinson states, "The Supreme Court decision had enough moral if not legal force to make impossible in the 1830s the abrogation of old treaties or the abandonment of treaty making."[63] Marshall's ruling established that it was the federal government, and not the states, who had the authority to negotiate with Indians. Following the *Worcester* decision, the nation almost universally came to accept the notion that the proper way to resolve Indian affairs was to negotiate treaties. Even Georgia stepped back and let the federal government dictate the final terms of the Cherokee removal. Since the time of the Cherokee-Georgia disputes, the United States has administered its policy to Indians strictly through the federal courts and the federal Bureau of Indian Affairs.

Marshall's definition of domestic dependent nations has left the twenty-first century with a unique and often confusing relationship between Native Americans and the United States. Many Indians are in most ways indistinguishable from any other citizens of the United States. They are active members of many U.S. communities, fight in the nation's armed forces, and hold office in the U.S. government. Yet many of them also continue to live on reserved lands administered by their own system of government, where they are exempt from state laws such as those banning casino gambling.

Native American Legal Rights

Marshall's decisions in the Cherokee cases established the legal principle that the Indians originally had full rights to their lands, and that any rights they did not voluntarily give away were re-

THE CHEROKEE TODAY

Like most Native American tribes, the Cherokee today struggle to overcome the poverty that has plagued them since the days of the removal. But the Cherokees' ability to adapt to cultural changes has continued to serve them in good stead. Geoffrey Norman, writing in *National Geographic*, says, "The transplanted Cherokees of Oklahoma—of all the Indian groups in North America—have probably succeeded the most in bridging the two disparate worlds in which, for better or worse, the twentieth century Indian must live."

Despite having no tribal territory of their own, the western Cherokee have stayed together as a distinct nation, now numbering more than 160,000. Since the 1970s, they have taken over almost all social programs that used to be run by the federal government. The tribe has assumed complete control of schools that were once controlled by the federal Bureau of Indian Affairs. Roughly thirteen-hundred workers at the W. W. Keeler Tribal Complex in northeastern Oklahoma carry out programs that assist with everything from employment to treatment for substance abuse to stocking lakes and streams with fish.

The western Cherokee have reestablished a capital at Tahlequah, Oklahoma. Their communities closely resemble those of whites, and many of them work in heavy industries. At the same time, they work hard to preserve traditional crafts, religious rites, dances, and the Cherokee language and history. As Wilma Mankiller, the only woman to serve as principal chief of the Cherokee Nation, observed, "We need to know what we have done before so that we can do it again."

Meanwhile a smaller band of Cherokee remains on nearly sixty thousand scattered acres of ancient Cherokee land in North Carolina. They have capitalized on their location as the gateway to the Great Smoky Mountains National Park, which attracts millions of visitors a year. Teepees, colorful headdresses, and storefronts splashed with artwork advertise their heritage as Indian and entice curious tourists into stopping at Cherokee towns. But while the tourism industry brings employment during the summer, the wages are not high. Off-season work is scarce. Like many tribes, the eastern Cherokee have sought to take advantage of their freedom from state control by creating a gaming industry with large jackpots.

tained. This included the right to self-government within their
lands. This issue has come up several times in federal court
cases, most notably that of *Ex Parte Crow Dog* in 1883. Crow Dog
was a Brule Sioux convicted of murdering the Sioux leader Spotted Tail on Sioux land. Federal prosecutors wanted to execute
Crow Dog for the crime as federal law allowed.

But Sioux tribal law called only for Crow Dog to compensate
the relatives of his victim. The dispute went to the Supreme
Court. Citing the Cherokee cases as the foundation for its opinion, the Court ruled nine to zero that the authority to punish
Crow Dog belonged to the Sioux. The case prompted Congress
to pass legislation specifying seven crimes, including murder,
over which the federal courts would have jurisdiction even in Indian territory. However, the federal courts have continued to uphold the *Worcester* principle of a tribe's right to self-governance
within its boundaries.

The most obvious recent result of the Cherokee cases has
been in the area of treaty rights. After nearly a century and a half
of lying dormant, issues of Indian treaty rights resurfaced in the
latter part of the twentieth century. Many tribes have become as-
sertive in claiming certain rights guaranteed to them under old
treaties with the United States. For example, the Chippewa in
Northern Wisconsin and Minnesota claimed that federal treaties
gave them the right to spear an unlimited number of spawning
gamefish, such as walleyes and muskies. Against the angry
protests of sport fishermen, the federal courts upheld the
Chippewa's rights. In Florida, Native Americans were spared
penalties for the killing of a Florida panther, a federally protected animal because it was killed on Native American land.
The foundation for these rulings was Marshall's opinion in
Worcester v. Georgia.

National Significance

Beyond its significance in defining Indian law, the *Worcester* decision ranks as one of the nation's most important legal cases because it was an exercise in political courage that helped solidify
the Supreme Court as a vital national institution. The tempta-

tion was great, in the face of tremendous pressure from President Jackson and the state of Georgia, for the justices to avoid the case. Marshall biographer Charles Hobson insists, "To have remained silent in the face of the state's violation of Constitutional and United States law would have damaged the Supreme Court's claim to be guardian of the law." Although its decision did not help the Cherokee, "it mattered greatly that the Court should be perceived as faithfully discharging its duties." [64]

In the words of historian Frances Paul Prucha, "Appeals to good faith and national honor had not fallen on deaf ears. [The justices'] training, experience, and, finally, their humanity—all of the things that blend into the rule of law—brought them up short when it came to signing an opinion that would have obliterated these promises." [65]

Not only was the Supreme Court's reputation on the line in these cases, but so was the nation's. A later Supreme Court justice, Hugo Black, would observe that "Great nations, like great men, should keep their word." [66] *Worcester* helped the United States to gain status before the countries of the world as a principled nation. The justices took a risk in making their stand. The Court came perilously close to provoking the president into a power struggle that could have gutted its authority. But even though Jackson did not actively enforce the Court's decision, he stopped short of claiming the right to defy or disregard its decisions. By holding its ground and risking (and surviving) the wrath of its critics, the Court eventually gained acceptance as the nation's final word in legal matters.

Notes

Introduction: A Question of Principles

1. Quoted in Samuel L. Carter III, *Cherokee Sunset: A Nation Betrayed.* New York: Doubleday, 1976, p. 108.
2. Quoted in Kermit L. Hall, ed., *The Oxford Companion to the Supreme Court of the United States.* New York: Oxford University Press, 1992, p. 580.

Chapter 1: Cherokee Land

3. Anthony F. C. Wallace, *The Long, Bitter Trail: Andrew Jackson and the Indians.* New York: Hill and Wang, 1993, p. 26.
4. Theda Perdue and Michael Green, eds., *The Cherokee Removal.* New York: Bedford Books, 1995, p. 9.
5. Quoted in Wallace, *The Long, Bitter Trail*, p. 32.
6. Quoted in Henry Watson, *Liberty and Power: The Politics of Jacksonian America.* New York: Noonday Press, 1996, p. 106.

Chapter 2: Federal Policy: Civilize or Relocate?

7. Quoted in Francis Paul Prucha, *American Indian Treaties: The History of a Political Anomaly.* Berkeley: University of California Press, 1994, p. 1.
8. Quoted in Louis Filler and Allen Guttmann, eds., *The Removal of the Cherokee Nation: Manifest Destiny or National Dishonor?* Boston: D. C. Heath, 1962, p. 14.
9. Quoted in Wallace, *The Long, Bitter Trail*, p. 61.
10. Quoted in Francis Paul Prucha, *Indian Policy in the United States.* Lincoln: University of Nebraska Press, 1981, p. 54.
11. Quoted in Watson, *Liberty and Power,* p. 110.
12. Quoted in Prucha, *Indian Policy*, p. 54.
13. Quoted in Wallace, *The Long, Bitter Trail*, p. 39.
14. Quoted in Carter, *Cherokee Sunset*, p. 103.
15. Quoted in Thurman Wilkens, *Cherokee Tragedy.* Norman: University of Oklahoma, 1970, p. 211.
16. Perdue and Green, *The Cherokee Removal,* , p. 61.
17. Quoted in Filler and Guttmann, *The Removal of the Cherokee Nation*, p. 22

18. Watson, *Liberty and Power,* p. 107.
19. Perdue and Green, *The Cherokee Removal,* p. 17.

Chapter 3: Cherokee Nation v. Georgia

20. Quoted in Perdue and Green, *The Cherokee Removal,* p. 61.
21. Quoted in John Ehle, *Trail of Tears: The Rise and Fall of the Cherokee Nation.* New York: Doubleday, 1988, p. 220.
22. Quoted in Watson, *Liberty and Power,* p. 109.
23. Quoted in Ehle, *Trail of Tears,* p. 235.
24. Quoted in Filler and Guttmann, *The Removal of the Cherokee Nation,* p. 7.
25. Quoted in Ehle, *Trail of Tears,* p. 235.
26. Quoted in Prucha, *American Indian Treaties,* p. 102.
27. Quoted in Charles F. Hobson, *The Great Chief Justice: John Marshall and the Rule of Law.* Lawrence: University of Kansas Press, 1996, p. 174.
28. Quoted in Carter, *Cherokee Sunset,* p. 106.
29. Quoted in Edward W. Knoppman, *Great American Trials.* Detroit: Gale Research, 1994, p. 88.
30. Quoted in Filler and Guttmann, *The Removal of the Cherokee Nation,* p. 27.
31. Quoted in Knoppman, *Great American Trials,* p. 89.
32. Carter, *Cherokee Sunset,* p. 104.
33. Quoted in Knoppman, *Great American Trials,* p. 88.
34. Quoted in Hobson, *The Great Chief Justice,* p. 175.
35. Quoted in Prucha, *American Indian Treaties,* p. 5.
36. Quoted in William C. Canby, *American Indian Law.* St. Paul, MN: West Publishing, 1981, p. 14.
37. Quoted in Canby, *American Indian Law,* p. 14.
38. Quoted in Filler and Guttmann, *The Removal of the Cherokee Nation,* p. 7.

Chapter 4: Worcester v. Georgia

39. Quoted in Hall, *The Oxford Companion to the Supreme Court of the United States,* p. 495.
40. Quoted in Hall, *The Oxford Companion to the Supreme Court of the United States,* p. 496.
41. Quoted in Hall, *The Oxford Companion to the Supreme Court of*

the United States, p. 496.

42. Quoted in Hall, *The Oxford Companion to the Supreme Court of the United States*, p. 496.
43. Hobson, *The Great Chief Justice*, p. 170.
44. Quoted in Ronald Satz, *American Indian Policy in the Jacksonian Era*. Lincoln: University of Nebraska Press, 1975, p. 46.
45. Quoted in Carter, *Cherokee Sunset*, p. 118.
46. Quoted in Hobson, *The Great Chief Justice*, p. 177.
47. Quoted in Perdue and Green, *The Cherokee Removal*, p. 73.
48. Quoted in Hobson, *The Great Chief Justice*, p. 178.
49. Quoted in Canby, *American Indian Law*, p. 15.
50. Quoted in Filler and Guttmann, *The Removal of the Cherokee Nation*, p. 11.
51. Quoted in Perdue and Green, *The Cherokee Removal*, p. 74.
52. Quoted in Canby, *American Indian Law*, p. 16.
53. Quoted in Wilkens, *Cherokee Tragedy*, p. 235.
54. Quoted in Henry J. Abraham, *Justices and Presidents*. New York: Oxford University Press, 1974, p. 86.

Chapter 5: Results of the Cherokee Cases

55. Satz, *American Indian Policy in the Jacksonian Era*, p. 49.
56. Quoted in Satz, *American Indian Policy in the Jacksonian Era*, p. 49.
57. Quoted in Wallace, *The Long, Bitter Trail*, p. 277.
58. Quoted in Filler and Guttmann, *The Removal of the Cherokee Nation*, p. 11.
59. Hobson, *The Great Chief Justice*, p. 179.
60. Wallace, *The Long, Bitter Trail*, p. 11.
61. Wallace, *The Long, Bitter Trail*, p. 11.
62. Prucha, *American Indian Treaties*, p. 167.
63. Quoted in Prucha, *American Indian Treaties*, p. 19.
64. Hobson, *The Great Chief Justice*, p. 180.
65. Prucha, *American Indian Treaties*, p. 167.
66. Quoted in Prucha, *American Indian Treaties*, p. 17.

For Further Reading

Alice Osinski, *Andrew Jackson*. Chicago: Childrens Press, 1987. This easy-reading book gives a picture of Andrew Jackson, the man most instrumental in carrying out the Cherokee removal.

Theda Perdue, *The Cherokee*. New York: Chelsea House, 1989. Perhaps the most thorough book written on a young adult reading level about the Cherokee. Perdue, who has also written several scholarly books on the same subject for adults, makes the information on the culture of the Cherokee accessible and includes detailed information about the Cherokee removal era.

Tamara L. Roleff, *Native American Rights*. San Diego: Greenhaven, 1998. This book, part of an extensive anthology series on current controversies, introduces the reader to a variety of viewpoints on the subject of contemporary Native American rights under federal laws and treaties.

Works Consulted

Henry J. Abraham, *Justices and Presidents*. New York: Oxford University Press, 1974. An overview of some of the political considerations involving presidents and the justices they named to the Supreme Court.

William C. Canby, *American Indian Law*. St. Paul, MN: West Publishing, 1981. A scholarly compilation of legal issues both past and present in U.S.–Native American relations.

Samuel L. Carter III, *Cherokee Sunset: A Nation Betrayed*. New York: Doubleday, 1976. A fairly straightforward history of the events surrounding the Cherokee removal.

John Ehle, *Trail of Tears: The Rise and Fall of the Cherokee Nation*. New York: Doubleday, 1988. Probably the best, most thorough, and most easily understood of the many books recounting the history of the Cherokee tribe. It includes many stories of individuals involved.

Louis Filler and Allen Guttmann, eds., *The Removal of the Cherokee Nation: Manifest Destiny or National Dishonor?* Boston: D. C. Heath, 1962. An excellent collection of primary sources that give a broad perspective of the views and attitudes that prevailed at the time of the removal.

Kermit L. Hall, ed., *The Oxford Companion to the Supreme Court of the United States*. New York: Oxford University Press, 1992. This has brief descriptions of the most influential Supreme Court cases, including the Cherokee cases.

Charles F. Hobson, *The Great Chief Justice: John Marshall and the Rule of Law*. Lawrence: University of Kansas Press, 1996. A probing look at a dominant force in American legal history, it has a chapter that goes into great detail about the workings of the Supreme Court and Marshall's deliberations on the Cherokee cases.

Edward W. Knoppman, *Great American Trials*. Detroit: Gale Research, 1994. This book on important trials in U.S. history includes a chapter on the Cherokee cases.

Theda Perdue and Michael Green, eds., *The Cherokee Removal*.

New York: Bedford Books, 1995. A detailed history of the events surrounding the removal.

Francis Paul Prucha, *American Indian Treaties: The History of a Political Anomaly.* Berkeley: University of California Press, 1994. This book focuses on the point that relations between Native Americans and the United States are unique in the history of international relations.

Francis Paul Prucha, *Indian Policy in the United States.* Lincoln: University of Nebraska Press, 1981. This book explores the entire history of U.S.–Native American relations. It explains not only how and why the policies developed but also how they have shaped the current state of affairs in the United States.

Ronald Satz, *American Indian Policy in the Jacksonian Era.* Lincoln: University of Nebraska Press, 1975. This study goes beyond some of the accepted surface wisdom to explain why Andrew Jackson did not enforce the Supreme Court's decision.

Anthony F. C. Wallace, *The Long, Bitter Trail: Andrew Jackson and the Indians.* New York: Hill and Wang, 1993. This book focuses on Andrew Jackson, his motivations and methods, as the prime mover behind the Indian removal.

Henry Watson, *Liberty and Power: The Politics of Jacksonian America.* New York: Noonday Press, 1996. This book covers the political situation and societal attitudes that prevailed at the time of the debates over Indian removal.

Thurman Wilkens, *Cherokee Tragedy.* Norman: University of Oklahoma, 1970. This takes a more personal look at the effects of the removal debates and policy, focusing primarily on how removal affected one prominent Cherokee family, the Ridges.

Index

Adams, John, 68
Adams, John Quincy, 40
agriculture, 11
alcohol, 8, 15
American Board of Commissioners
  for Foreign Missions, 50, 65, 75
Ani-Yunwiya. *See* Cherokee
assimilation
  of Cherokee, 37
  Indian reform movement and,
    30–32
  Knox and, 30

Baldwin, Henry, 61, 69
beaver, 14
Black, Hugo, 85
Boudinot, Elias
  on efforts to remove Cherokee,
    48–49
  founding of *Cherokee Phoenix* and,
    37, 38
  missionaries and, 65
  murder of, 80
Butler, Elizur, 64, 69, 70, 75

Calhoun, John, 36, 78
Carp, Robert, 68
Carter, Samuel, III, 54
Cass, Lewis, 36
Cherokee
  Civil War and, 80
  culture of, 11, 23, 26, 31–32
  current situation of, 83
  economy of, 11, 14–16
  effects of *Worcester v. Georgia* on, 76,
    77
  as foreign nation, 54, 58
  government of, 37
  population of, 19–20, 80–81, 83
  removal of, 36, 77–80
  status in Georgia of, 7
  territory of, 11
  warfare
    abandonment of, 25–26
    with colonists, 18, 19
    with other Native American
      tribes, 11–12, 16, 23, 26
    with pioneers, 25

Cherokee Nation v. Georgia
  arguments in, 53–55
  decision in, 55–57
  dissent in, 58–59
  effects of, 58, 82–85
  precedent-setting nature of, 9–10
Cherokee Phoenix (newspaper)
  on efforts to remove Cherokee,
    48–49
  founding of, 37, 38, 62
  on *Worcester v. Georgia* decision, 70
Cherokee Removal, The (Perdue and
  Green, eds.), 39
Chickasaw, 21, 23
Chippewa, 77, 84
Choctaw
  culture of, 23
  treaties with United States, 21
  warfare against Cherokee, 11
Civil War, 80
claim of conquest
  Johnson v. McIntosh and, 55
  Proclamation of 1763 and, 18
  Revolutionary War and, 19
  states and, 20
  United States and, 21–22
Clay, Henry, 78
Clayton, A. S., 46
Clayton, Augustin, 63
Constitution
  commerce with Native Americans
    and, 23
  treaties and, 22
Continental Congress, 20
cotton, 33–34
Creek
  culture of, 23
  removal of, 76
  sale of land by, 42
  warfare against Cherokee, 11, 23,
    26
Creek War, 23, 26, 49
Crockett, Davy, 49
Crow Dog, 84

Declaration of Independence, 35
deer, 15
discovery, right of

Europe and, 13–14, 27
Johnson v. McIntosh and, 55
United States and, 22, 27
Worcester v. Georgia and, 66
diseases, 12–13
domestic dependent nations, 56, 67, 82
Duval, Gabriel, 61, 69

England
colonization and, 13–15, 16, 18
French and Indian War and, 16–18
missionaries and, 65
Native American policy of, 16, 18
Revolutionary War and, 18–19, 20
Evarts, Jeremiah, 50
Everett, Edward, 44
Ex Parte Crow Dog, 84

farming, 11
Five Civilized Tribes, 23
Forsyth, John, 32, 36
France
French and Indian War and, 16–18
Native American policy of, 17
Frelinghuysen, Theodore, 44, 49
French and Indian War, 16–18
furs, 14, 15

Georgia
courts of, 46
land deal with United States, 24
laws of
missionaries and, 60
Native Americans and, 46, 47
concerning land, 42, 46
creation of Georgia Guard, 43
gold mining, 44
outlawing Cherokee
government, 43
status of Cherokee and, 7, 8
Supreme Court and, 66
Worcester v. Georgia and, 69, 70
Georgia Guard
Cherokee and, 8, 43–44, 47
missionaries and, 62–63
Gilmer (governor of Georgia), 9, 63
Gist, Nathaniel, 38
gold, 7–8, 43
Great Britain
colonization and, 13–15, 16, 18

French and Indian War and, 16–18
missionaries and, 65
Native American policy of, 16, 18
Revolutionary War and, 18–19, 20
Greenville, Treaty of, 25
Guess, George, 38

Hobson, Anthony, F. C., 59
Hobson, Charles, 85
Holston, Treaty of, 21, 54
Hopewell, Treaty of, 21, 24
Horseshoe Bend, Battle of, 26
hunting, 11, 15–16

Indian reform movement
opposition to, 32–34
support for, 30–32
Indian Removal Act, 44, 45, 46, 49
Indian removal movement, 32–34, 39, 43
voluntary removal and, 35–37
Indian Territory of Oklahoma, 36, 80
intermarriage, 32

Jackson, Andrew
background of, 45
Creek War and, 26
on Indian removal, 43, 45
response to Georgia laws
concerning Native Americans, 43
states' rights and, 41, 47–48, 68
Treaty of New Echota and, 78
view of Native Americans 40–41
Worcester v. Georgia and, 71, 73–75, 85
Jefferson, Thomas
on assimilation of Native
Americans, 30
removal of Native Americans and, 34–35
states' rights and, 68
view of Native Americans, 35
Johnson, William, 61, 69
Johnson v. McIntosh, 55
Junaluska (Cherokee warrior), 26

Knox, Henry, 27–30

land
ownership of
Cherokee concept of, 11, 16, 37

claim of conquest and, 18, 19, 20,
21–22
in Indian Territory, 80
Johnson v. McIntosh and, 55
right of discovery and, 13–14, 22,
27
sale of, 22, 23, 24
by Cherokee, 76, 77–78
by Creek, 42
Native American concept of, 24–25
policy of Knox, 29
see also Indian Removal Act; Indian
removal movement
language, written, 37, 38
liquor, 8, 15
Louisiana Territory, 34
Lumpkin, Wilson
attitude toward missionaries, 60
on removal of Cherokee, 39
on states' rights, 54

Mankiller, Wilma, 83
Marshall, John
background of, 51–52, 68
Cherokee Nation v. Georgia and
decision in, 55–57, 59–60, 82–85
dissent in, 59
Johnson v. McIntosh and, 55
on relations between Native
Americans and United States, 27
Supreme Court and
effect on, 68, 75–76
view of role of, 52
Worcester v. Georgia and, 66–67,
68–69
Martin v. Hunter's Lessee, 61
McLean, John, 61, 69, 76
measles, 12–13
Mille Lacs, Lake, 77
missionaries, 60, 62–65
Indian reform movement and,
30–31
Monroe, James, 36, 39–40
Morse, Jedidiah, 30

National Geographic (magazine), 83
Native Americans
attitudes toward, 32
as domestic dependent nations, 56,
67, 82
as foreign nations, 54, 66, 67

legal rights of, 83–84
New Echota, 37
Treaty of, 77–78
Norman, Geoffrey, 83
Northwest Ordinance, 21, 22
nullification movement, 72–73

O'Connor, Sandra Day, 77
Osceola, 23

Proclamation of 1763, 18
Prucha, Frances Paul, 85

Red Sticks, 23
religion, 17, 37
see also missionaries
Revolutionary War, 18–20, 29
right of discovery
Europe and, 13–14, 27
Johnson v. McIntosh and, 55
United States and, 22, 27
Worcester v. Georgia and, 66
Ross, John, 46–47, 78

Sargent, John, 64
Satz, Ronald, 73
Scott, Winfield, 79
Seminole, 23
Sequoyah, 37, 38
Seven Years War, 17
Sharp Knife. *See* Jackson, Andrew
smallpox, 12–13
Sogwali (Sequoyah), 38
South Carolina, 72–73
Spotted Tail, 84
states' rights
Indian territory and, 20, 22, 72
Jackson and, 47–48
nullification and, 72–73
Supreme Court and, 54, 61
Stidham, Ronald, 68
Story, Joseph
background of, 61
Cherokee Nation v. Georgia and, 58,
59
Worcester v. Georgia and, 69
Supreme Court
Cherokee Nation v. Georgia
arguments in, 53–55
decision in, 55–57
dissent in, 58–59

effects of, 58, 82–85
precedent-setting nature of, 9–10
Chippewa suit and, 77
enforcement of decisions of, 70–71, 72, 76
Marshall and, 68, 75–76
Ex Parte Crow Dog and, 84
Johnson v. McIntosh and, 55
justices of, 61, 69, 77
see also Marshall, John
Marshall's view of, 52
Martin v. Hunter's Lessee, 61
original jurisdiction of, 53
powers of, 8, 85
Worcester v. Georgia
arguments in, 64–66
decision in, 66–67, 68–69
effects of, 76, 77, 82
justices in, 61

tariffs, 72–73
Tassels, George, 7, 9, 50
Thompson, Smith
background of, 61
Cherokee Nation v. Georgia and, 58–59
Worcester v. Georgia and, 69
trade, 14–15
Trail of Tears, The, 79–80
treaties
Cherokee Nation v. Georgia and, 58
as proof of nationhood, 54, 56, 66, 67
provisions of, 7, 8
between states and Native Americans, 20
between United States and Great Britain, 20
between United States and Native Americans, 20, 21, 40
Greenville, 25
Holston, 21, 54
Hopewell, 21, 24
New Echota, 77–78
violations of, 24
Worcester v. Georgia and, 82

United Church Board for World Missions, 65
United States
policy toward Native Americans, 29
Northwest Ordinance and, 21, 22
see also land, sale of; treaties

Van Buren, Martin, 74, 78–79
Ventura, Jesse, 77

Wallace, Anthony F. C.
on Cherokee removal, 80
on conditions in Indian Territory of Oklahoma, 80
on relations between Native Americans and colonists, 18
warfare
abandonment of, by Cherokee, 25–26
between Cherokee and colonists, 18, 19
hunting and, 16
between Native Americans and pioneers, 25
between Native American tribes, 11–12, 16, 23, 26
Washington, George, 17
Watson, Henry L., 41
Webster, Daniel, 78
whiskey, 8, 15
Wilkinson, Charles, 82
Wirt, William
background of, 50
Cherokee Nation v. Georgia and
on precedent-setting nature of, 9–10
strategy in, 50, 52–53
Worcester v. Georgia and, 64, 76
Worcester, Samuel, 62–64, 65, 69, 70
Worcester v. Georgia
arguments in, 64–66
decision in, 66–67, 68–69
effects of, 76, 77, 82
justices in, 61
Wureth (mother of Sequoyah), 38
W. W. Keeler Tribal Complex, 83

Picture Credits

About the Author

Nathan Aaseng is the author of more than 140 books for young readers on a wide variety of subjects. More than three dozen of his works have won awards. A former microbiologist with a degree in biology and English from Luther College (Iowa), he currently lives in Eau Claire, Wisconsin, with his wife and four children.